Alicia has been coach___ ___ 'ss than a year and has already led an amazing and deeply-felt positive transformation. She coaches with broad wisdom and empathy, is in tune with the latest understandings across the diversity of our organization and she uniquely creates safe space for dialog while simultaneously pulling you out of your comfort zone. Our organization is better because of her time with us.

—Steven VanRoekel
COO, The Rockefeller Foundation

Alicia has helped me transform in various leadership roles. Her insight and guidance has been critical towards my rapid development in my role as a founder and CEO. Alicia combines expertise in organizational change and personal effectiveness to address almost any issue I bring to her and at the same time pushes me outside my comfort zone, and challenges me to be a better leader.

—Suzanne Yoon
Founder & CEO, Kinzie Capital Management

Alicia's keen eye for opportunity and breadth of experience has been tremendously helpful as I navigate Backroads in a fast moving environment. She is always able to uncover dimensions of a problem or opportunity that stimulate worthwhile thought. Alicia's insight is simply invaluable.

—Tom Hale
Founder & CEO, Backroads

With Alicia's support I am a more effective and humble leader. Alicia can take someone who is very self aware to a whole new level. When she works with my direct reports it makes them feel valued and it has proven to be a great retention tool. She sets a tone in our culture for individuals to be open, innovate, take risks, value diversity, and reach beyond their natural set of aptitudes to become more whole contributors to the team.

—Katrina Markoff
Founder & CEO, Vosges Haut-Chocolat

Alicia is very passionate about her clients' success and takes a great interest in multiple aspects of their growth. Her feedback is direct, timely, and most importantly, practical.

—John Holmes
Group Vice President, Aviation Supply Chain, AAR

I have relied on Alicia for professional mentorship, support, and guidance for years. From brainstorming new program ideas to no-holds-barred reality checks and sage career advice, Alicia has been a great professional resource for me.

—Evelyn Diaz, CEO, Heartland Alliance

I have never been a fan of executive coaching, but I'm a convert after working with Alicia. She has keen insight into human motivation and psyche based on experience and analysis, and the ability to quickly translate that insight into action. I saw meaningful improvement after her involvement, and continue to work with her to get the best out of my executive team.

—Boris Elisman
Chairman and CEO, ACCO Brands Corporation

I call Alicia my business shrink but that actually understates the value she has created for me. She is my shrink, muse, connector, and encourager. She can – with intelligence, insight and clarity -- help you think through and devise a strategy (and, more than that, behaviors) to address the issues that stand in the way of success. She is possessed of a rare emotional intelligence, a keen, observational mind, and an uncanny ability to deliver criticism smartly and in a way the recipient can digest and act on.

—Rob Densen, Founder & CEO Tiller
Board Member PhilmCO Media

Alicia is extremely thoughtful, supportive and always action-oriented. She knows exactly how to push my thinking forward, and I truly believe her insights will continue to be instrumental in reaching a turning point during the most difficult periods in my career as well as personal life. Every conversation with her leaves me more empowered than I was before. She is a true mentor and role model in many ways.

—Joo-Yong Chung
Director, MBK Partners

Receiving feedback from Alicia is a gift. Her feedback is fact-based, direct, insightful, and actionable. She doesn't sugar coat feedback yet there is a kindness and support in the approach that is both inspiring and empowering. I seek out her insights regularly.

—Kelly McNamara-Corley
Member, Goldman Sachs Board

Alicia is uniquely effective at pushing even seasoned executives out of their comfort zones towards higher level performance as individuals and as part of a more highly functioning executive team.
—David Nelms, Chairman & CEO, Discover Financial Services

AND THE CLOUD YELLED BACK

AND THE CLOUD YELLED BACK

Clearing the Overcast on Leadership

ARTICLES, ESSAYS & COMMENTARIES

ALICIA BASSUK

UBICA

Table of Conents

Foreword

I MET ALICIA BASSUK SEVERAL YEARS ago and was immediately impressed by her innovative approach to leadership coaching. As a C-Suite legal professional, working in the financial services industry for over 36 years, my traditional leadership focus was on developing strong risk management.

After the financial crisis of 2007-2008, the financial services industry experienced an onslaught of new industry regulation. At the same time, new agile competitors entered the market, and technology was changing everything about the way our business operated. I turned to Alicia to help me focus on innovation and enhance team cohesion, as a way to manage through these changes and drive strong results.

During our very first phone call, and in just a few minutes of discussion, Alicia helped me develop a breakthrough approach to a management problem that had been vexing me for weeks.

Not only do I turn to Alicia to help sharpen my own leadership approach, she has worked with my team to enhance teamwork, engagement and strengthen skills around empathy, innovation, initiative, decision-making and judgment. While we were striving for best-in-class performance for our business, we also had the honor of being recognized with professional awards for innovation, results, diversity & inclusion and community service. The results spoke for themselves, and soon our Executive Leadership team was also tapping into Alicia's insights.

Alicia's passion for helping to develop strong, inclusive leaders and cohesive teams has profoundly impacted my leadership style, and her insights shine through on every page of this important book. Through this series of articles, Alicia offers clear leadership tips and techniques to help individuals and organizations operate at their peak potential. Her messages will resonate clearly with anyone striving to innovate, stretch and grow.

I've read all of these essays—some of them, many times! Each time I gain a new insight that helps me both personally and professionally. So, get ready to change gears. Get ready to be inspired. Get ready to be challenged to think about leadership in a new and refreshing way!

Kelly McNamara Corley
Board Member, Goldman Sachs

Introduction

"THE OLD MAN AND THE KEY" is the thirteenth episode, from the thirteenth season of the animated sitcom, *The Simpsons*. The triskaidekaphobia redundancy might be a psychic's reason the episode did not fare well with critics. But it did yield a memorable scene that launched a memorable meme—just to borrow upon the nautical theme of the Hemmingway title the episode borrowed from.

Do an internet search for "Old man yells at cloud", if you're not familiar with it. The pop culture meaning of it is a vain, cantankerous expression of one's indomitable absurdity. But when it comes to interpretations, perspectives matter. Personal frame of reference definitely frames a personal understanding of the world that can differ from the mainstream comprehension of things. My interpretation of that scene, and its meme, yielded quite a different meaning extracted from a view of the world, which often seemed different from conventional perspectives.

When that episode aired in 2002, I had just entered my thirties. The tenth year of building and growing my business was approaching. I was divorced with two daughters, whom I was raising as a solo parent. I was also deeply rooted with the personal industry work ethic seeded by my immigrant parents, who overcame the test of roach-infested living spaces and the prejudices that welcomed them to this country. Equally significant, I had three decades of honing my independent thinking, prompted by a mother awakened by the feminism of the 1970s, and liberated from the machismo of the Latino culture she was reared in.

The Civil Rights Movement of the 1960s had not become an echo in the lessons of my childhood. My middle-school years were scored by Madonna, and I had not yet graduated from Wesleyan when the Anita Hill hearings took place. I heard women like Barbara Boxer and Diane Feinstein step up to the political microphone, while listening to the gender-empowering sounds of Queen Latifah, Salt-N-Pepa and Mary J. Blige. And I watched Oprah Winfrey take over television.

So, by 2002, my personal frame of reference had framed an understanding of society and culture, that saw the need for more input and involvement from many people who had long been overshadowed by the "cloud" of bias, that was still looming over the more inclusive aspiration for a more perfect union.

It may be a stretch of reasoning to some, but when I saw the old man yelling at the cloud, I saw the old dictate of this country angrily exposing the foolishness of rejecting the certainty of change, a certainty I felt motivated and obligated to realize.

I reasoned I could impact that change by contributing to the development of leaders who were willing to see diversity as an opportunity instead of an obligation; leaders who would realize the true meaning of "from many comes one". To that end, I decided to write.

I decided it was time for the cloud to yell back.

Alicia Bassuk

7 Tricky Work Situations and How to Respond To Them

Harvard Business Review 10/11/17

YOU KNOW THE MOMENT: A mood-veering, thought-steering, pressure-packed interaction with a colleague, boss, or client where the right thing to say is stuck in a verbal traffic jam between your brain and your mouth.

Sian Beilock, president of Barnard College and author of Choke, found that this analysis paralysis occurs when your brain suddenly becomes overtaxed by worry or pressure. Consequently, you find yourself unable to respond to a mental, psychological, or emotional challenge, and you fail to execute in the critical moment.

Many people experience this at work. But there are certain phrases you can keep in your back pocket when these moments come. Route your response with them, and redirect the situation to regain control.

Situation #1: Someone takes credit for your idea.

Katie is the COO of a hospitality company. She has a keen strategic mind. In a contentious moment, she recommends that the C-suite move toward a new talent strategy. The idea is met with resistance. Then Dave, the head of IT, restates her idea in his own words. The rest of the C-suite supports him in "his" idea.

It's not a matter of *if* this situation happens, but *when*: You competently make a point. It goes unacknowledged or is tersely rejected. Minutes or days later, a colleague or manager misrepresents your point as their own, restates it identically, and is praised and credited for making it.

What you should say: "Thanks for spotlighting my point."

Why it works: Spoken with composure, it:

- prevents you from being trivialized by serving notice about the misappropriation of your contribution
- allows you to reclaim your idea without aspersion
- gives you the upper hand when addressing the matter with a manager
- provides an opportunity for greater ownership, if delivered in front of others, by offering detail or clarification for impact

6

Katie didn't skip a beat. "Thanks for spotlighting my point, Dave. There are a couple other topics worth considering in tandem with this. I'll review those quickly and we can delve into more detail in the next meeting." The group refocused their attention on Katie, and moved along to viewing her as the point person for the conversation.

Situation #2: You're asked to stay late when you're about to leave the office for a personal obligation.

Heather is a physician at a large urban hospital. Wednesdays at 4 PM she attends a one-hour clinic administration meeting. If Heather leaves by 5 PM she arrives home in time to allow the nanny to get to her own children's after-school program on time. At 5 PM, Heather stands up to leave. One of the clinic administrators asks if she can stay a few more minutes until they are done. Heather dreads saying she has to leave to relieve the nanny, because she knows her colleagues may judge her as having a poor work ethic.

What you should say: "Excuse me, I have another commitment."

Picking up your child from daycare, moving a parent into a care facility, or attending a surgery consultation with a dear friend are time sensitive, must-do things—especially when someone you love is depending on you. No matter how family-friendly a workplace claims to be, explaining family matters to colleagues can cause resentment.

7

Why it works: This sentence will minimize your risk of backlash because it:

- serves as an implicit, respectable request for confidentiality
- establishes an information boundary that puts anyone who crosses it at risk of appearing intrusive
- eliminates oversharing about the reason for your departure

Gathering her laptop and bag, Heather said, "Excuse me, I have another commitment." Another physician asked, "Where are you off to? Anything fun?" Walking toward the conference room door, Heather grabbed her water bottle with the parting phrase, "It's just something I committed to long before this meeting was scheduled. I'll swing by tomorrow to get caught up."

Situation #3: In a pivotal situation, a trusted colleague snaps at you.

Manuel and Alvin run their website out of their home. Manuel writes content. Alvin designs and formats. Manuel realizes Alvin's work often requires longer hours to tend to. In appreciation, he frequently buys Alvin lunch, occasionally gifts him chiropractic treatments for chronic back problems, and sometimes surprises him with an addition to his wardrobe. One day Alvin approaches Manuel and tells him he wants to make a major career shift. Manuel says nothing. Feeling ignored, Alvin repeats his intention and asks, "You have nothing to say about this?" Dismissively, Manuel responds, "About what?" Alvin feels disrespected by Manuel's lack of concern or consideration. Despite Manuel's many acts of appreciation, Alvin regularly feels shortchanged in comparison with the focus, regard, and responsiveness Manuel shows to paying customers. When Alvin addresses it, Manuel snaps back, "Look at how much I do for you!"

What you should say: "This isn't about what you do *for* me. It is about what you did *to* me."

You know when a valued colleague, someone who almost always does right by you, damages your good rapport? Frustration follows when your attempt to address it is met with a retort and a guilt trip. Though their concerns may be valid, it doesn't mean they should be rude.

Why it works: When stated without emotional inflammation, this sentence can quickly reduce frustrations by:

- limiting the scope of the exchange to the isolated misstep, and not being derailed by an exchange about a history of mutual consideration
- quickly dealing with the fact-based, cause-effect dynamics of the exchange
- allowing for an opportunity to establish mutually affirming conduct going forward

Alvin took a deep breath. "This isn't about what you do for *me. It is about what you did* to *me." He went on to acknowledge Manuel's appreciation for his work, and then addressed his partner's unresponsiveness. Manuel apologized, realizing he hurt*

9

Alvin by not being more mindful and considerate when Alvin came to speak to him.

Situation #4: You have to say "no."

Sam sends Julia a text at 9 PM on Saturday night, with an idea that could give the company an edge in customer service's call hold times. Julia has been asked to work more collaboratively with Sam, but she has been avoiding it because Sam is unreliable.

What you should say: "This is a good launching point."

Saying no is tough to do, especially when trying to demonstrate you are hardworking and a team player. It often seems easier to say yes to appease others, flash the right optics, or get the task out of the way.

Why it works: Spoken with a tone of enthusiasm and flexibility, this positive statement allows you to bow out of the initial request, while protecting your reputation by:

- reframing their idea as a starting point
- allowing you to entertain the request without committing to it
- creating the option to shape the request
- doling out diplomacy not rejection

Julia texted Sam "This is a good launching point! I'll get my team together to prepare the data, and reach out to you with ideas of how we can approach the call hold times."

Situation #5: You have to give negative or awkward feedback to someone you're close with.

Tony is a purchaser at a chocolate factory. For two years Jay has been both his manager and his friend. Lately, many other employees have asked Jay to tell Tony that he has halitosis. The situation has become intolerable for many, even off-putting to vendors.

What you should say: "I'm here to be for you what someone once was for me."

When you are giving sensitive feedback, no matter how much you try to position yourself as an advocate, people tend to become defensive. It makes you question if giving the feedback is even worth it.

Why it works: Delivered in a calm and candid tone, this sentence can save a career, or life-altering moment, from becoming a decimating event with an alienating outcome by:

- giving the other person a moment to brace themselves
- leading by sharing a personal account of a tough feedback situation you experienced, which endorses the value of receiving and listening to criticism
- instantly unifying you with the other person through your shared vulnerability
- shifting them from hearing the message as disparagement to hearing it as encouragement or concern

Jay approached Tony at his desk and let him know he had some quick feedback. "Tony, I'm here to be for you what someone once was for me. You may have noticed that I take a step back when we talk. I and others have experienced, on several occasions, that your breath isn't always the best. It could just be dehydration, but I'm concerned it could indicate something you might want to discuss with your dentist or doctor." He handed Tony a pack of breath mints. Tony, though a bit embarrassed, smiled and thanked him. Jay shook Tony's hand and headed back to his desk.

Situation #6: You need to push back on a decision you believe is wrong.

Mae-Li is a partner and the head of the most important research team at a pharmaceutical company. Her team is the only group in the company that is almost entirely Chinese and majority female. When the office is undergoing a redesign, a few top managers are tapped to decide which groups will be moved to the less desirable basement level. Without asking for her input, Mae-Li's group is selected to move to the basement. She feels slighted.

What you should say: "This is my preference."

Sometimes, when something bothers you, addressing it can leave you feeling apprehensive and conflicted. You can spend time analyzing and detailing a defense for your perspective, but it may just overcomplicate matters.

Why it works: It will allow you to direct the conversation toward a desired change, while still conveying openness for other approaches by:

- clearly communicating your concern and what you want
- reasoning rather than offering a defiant dictate
- demonstrating you are willing to get involved with a potentially sensitive topic
- giving others the heads-up that the outcome matters to you enough to track it as it develops

Mae-Li popped her head into her manager's office. She explained that since she wasn't consulted by the moving committee before being directed to move, she wanted to share her perspective, in the hope that her manager would share it with the committee. "I realize that some of the teams are going to have to move, but it's unclear why mine was selected for the basement. I want my team to stay on this floor. This is my preference." Her manager took notes, confirmed Mae-Li's perspective, and let her know that he would advocate for her team.

Situation #7: You need to escalate a serious issue.

Eva is an engineer in Silicon Valley. While away at an industry event in New York, she returns to her hotel to find her manager in the hotel lobby. He tells her that he flew there to spend time with her because he has strong feelings for her. When Eva reports this to Abe from the HR department, he tells her that her manager is one of the top performers at the company, that he has been there for many years without incident, and that she probably misinterpreted what he said.

What you should say: "Your response gives me cause to take this further."

13

When it comes to serious issues like sexual harassment, there is still inconsistency with how managers and HR departments handle complaints. This can leave you worried and troubled about being mistreated again, about losing opportunities for promotion, and even about losing your job.

Why it works: This serious statement, delivered in a calm and matter-of-fact tone, informs the offender and managers that you will not be complicit and compliant with misconduct, and that you will figure out a way to take further action, by:

- establishing that the issue isn't going away, whether they elect to handle the situation themselves or answer to someone else about it later
- being transparent about your plan to escalate
- demonstrating that you expect the offender to suffer consequences for committing the poor conduct, and that you will not suffer consequences for reporting it
- empowering you in the moment, rather than demoralizing you in the aftermath

Eva was not deterred by Abe's response. She wrote his words verbatim in her notebook and said, "I shared the facts with you. Your response gives me cause to take this further." Abe raised his eyebrows and asked, "Are you sure this is a battle worth fighting with your manager?" Eva again wrote Abe's words verbatim in her notebook. She responded, "Yes, I'm sure," and repeated, "Your response gives me cause to take this further." She thanked Abe and left the office to email another executive at the company, with the intent to pursue redress.

NBA Gender Equity

Medium 3/24/19

THE NBA'S FEBRUARY 2019 ALL-STAR Weekend bash in Charlotte staged events on and off the court. Most were designed to be entertaining, others enlightening. Of course, there was the celebrity game, the three-point shooting contest, the dunk contest, musical performances, fashion, art and interactive activities offered to enhance the fan experience.

Other events took on a dimension of social impact. The National Basketball Wives Association (NBWA) presented The Women's Empowerment Summit, honoring the Evolution of Women in Business. It also, along with the March of Dimes, co-sponsored a baby shower for low income mothers. Aside from gifting strollers, car seats and clothes, the shower served the greater purpose of outreach, to expectant mothers at higher risk of dying during pregnancy.

There was also a focus on gender equity in the league. The Female Quotient (FQ), a female-owned business with a staunch commitment for advancing equality in the workplace, hosted the FQ Equality Lounge, which served as a forum for women to connect and collaborate.

The Thursday before All-Star Weekend festivities began, The FQ Equality Lounge conducted the Women in Basketball Operations forum, the goal of which is to develop female leaders and executives for basketball operations roles. The forum was supported and attended by NBA Commissioner Adam Silver, who acknowledges the gender imbalance in senior NBA roles. He also realizes that the disparity will not improve, without the proactive hiring intention of the league's decision makers—the owners, presidents and general managers, who are predominantly men. To Silver's credit, he is creating an infrastructure to build upon that intention. To that end, he asked various attendees at the forum, for ideas about how to position more women in the pipeline for roles as General Manager and Head Coach.

Two weeks later, at the MIT/Sloan Sports Analytics Conference in Boston, Commissioner Silver sat for an interview with Bill Simmons of *The Ringer*. During the hour-long discussion, Silver spoke comprehensively and insightfully about free agency and player leverage, the changes in contract structures through the decades, the role and future of the G-League, audience viewing habits, league expansion, global development of the game—an A-Z topic list regarding all things NBA. There was a glaring omission of one letter, in that topic alphabet. It was surprising given Silver's comments about gender equity in the NBA, just two weeks prior at the All-Star game. There was no "W".

Not once did Silver or Simmons mention the words "woman" or "women". This means there was no discussion about increasing the ranks of women in the NBA, in basketball operations and coaching. It also means there was no mention of the WNBA, a league started by the NBA with the promotional merit of gender equity. This is noteworthy given the ongoing gender equity issues WNBA players clamor to be addressed: salaries, training facilities, travel arrangements, marketing and endorsement opportunities. The word "girls" did come up, when Silver spoke about improving youth development so "boys and girls" are better equipped to handle the consequences of anxiety and loneliness, concerns Silver very recently brought attention to.

Basketball is not a sport played, cheered, understood, taught, talked about, wagered on, followed, loved, coached, viewed and economically supported only by men. There's not a continent on the planet (Antarctica, maybe) where girls and women are not dribbling, passing, shooting, rebounding, displeased with referees and yes, even dunking. From its inception in 1891, when Dr. James Naismith invented the game, basketball has developed as a sport for women and men simultaneously.

If that's not enough for Silver, Simmons and others to give equitable credence to, they might consider this.

Mothers are generally the parent who pays the fees and signs the permission slips, for their daughters and sons to play at schools and park district field houses across the country. Mothers are largely responsible for transporting their daughters and sons to and from practices and games. Mothers are most often relied on to escort their aspiring athletes to sporting goods stores, to buy the shoes and equipment they play with, and the athletic apparel that must be laundered later. Mothers are generally the parent signing up their future Breanna Stewarts and Steph Currys for clinics and camps and tournaments. Mothers are counted on most to never miss a game. Mothers instill confidence in their young competitors that leads them to victories, and console the psyches of their defeated brood when they suffer losses. In short, from birth to draft night, whether it's the WNBA or the NBA, mothers create the players Silver and Simmons rely on. Mothers also represent a $2.4 trillion demographic market. Men who run the business and media of the league can periodically watch Kevin Durant's tearful expression of gratitude to his mother when accepting the MVP award, to realize who the real MVP is.

A few days after the conference in Boston, ESPN posted a Players Only video called *In the League*. It features women in the NBA talking about what it means to be a woman working in a male-dominated sport. While the NBA boasts a handful of women executives, trainers and assistant coaches, the mantle of General Manager or Head Coach still remains an all-male domain.

The last team presented in the video, the Toronto Raptors, offers some hope of continued progress. The Raptors featured five women on the team's employee roster. A quote from team president Masai Ujiri provides insight as to why Toronto is more progressive than other teams, as well as instructional insight for the league about how it can be: "People see [hiring women] as an obligation. It is not that to me. It's an opportunity." The risk in not viewing it as such is that gender equity can be viewed as a socially conscious marketing lure for female fans, rather than an earnest initiative with real intent and application. Female fans number in the millions—millions. That's an audience to propagate not patronize.

Girls' and women's sports teams, from elementary school to the Olympics to the professional level, have long been overshadowed by men as coaches, officials, administrators, executives and owners. That men can be presumed to have a competent and credible stewardship of teams and leagues for women but not vice versa, goes beyond being a rational disconnect. It speaks to sexist sophistry. This is most insultingly ironic given that historically many women in sports have been trained, coached, taught and mentored by men. Jeanie Buss and every woman who has played for the UCONN Huskies since 1985 are superb examples.

A comparable sophistry exists relative to race. For athletes of color, who in some cases dominate certain sports, to not be hired as head coaches and executives in proportion to their representation as players, while their white counterparts are being hired at an inverse proportion to their representation ratio, speaks not to the ineptitude of athletes of color but to the exclusion of white owners and executives who control professional sports. African American players comprise roughly 75% of team rosters, in the NBA. At the start of the 2018–2019 season, 494 players filled roster spots, 367 of whom were African American. However, the NBA has only 8 African American men as head coaches and 7 African American men in positions of president or general manager—the only minorities influencing decision making from the front office, in the entire NBA. Juxtapose this against the reality that the predominantly African American NBPA, the union for NBA players, hired Michele Roberts, an African American woman, to be its Executive Director and a discrepancy in intent becomes flagrantly obvious.

Each year, NBA coaches and executives are hired, fired and replaced. The end of the 2018–2019 season resulted in one of the highest coaching and GM turnovers in history: 9 head coaches and 3 general managers. Despite the league's touting of Becky Hammond being interviewed for head coach by the Milwaukee Bucks,—the first woman to ever be interviewed for that position by any team in the league, men were hired to fill all of those vacancies. The recycling carousel of failed male coaches and front office directors continues, gender equity marketing aside.

The NBA has been pointing an incriminating finger at itself about this, for the past two decades. The league approved formation of the WNBA in 1996, with the first season beginning the following year in 1997. That same year, a Chicago Tribune op-ed, by freelance writer and basketball fan Michael Tyler, criticized the double-standard which posits that men can coach women in the WNBA, but women can't coach men in the NBA. The article suggested legendary University of Tennessee Lady Volunteers Head Coach Pat Summit as an unassailable NBA candidate. It states that "relative to instruction of fundamentals, talent assessment, development of plays, game strategy and orchestration of staff", Summit has proven herself. That Becky Hammond is the first and only woman to garner a head coach interview from the NBA, 23 years after the inception of the WNBA, charts the reluctant pace of progress of the league.

The topic of hiring women in the NBA has to become part of a constant and continuous conversation, if an obvious, significant, culture-shifting impact on gender equity is to be achieved by the league. This point is one Masai Ujiri brings up during his interview for *In the League*. Though input and participation from women is vital for realizing gender equity, this conversation needs to occur more between the men who govern and comprise the league—the owners, the Commissioner, the presidents, the general managers and the players. Why?

History is clear about the pursuit of enfranchisement by a disenfranchised people. Pleas, petitions and protests for inclusion are first and repeatedly rejected by those with the power of redress. This has been true for the great campaigns of history: the abolition of slavery, the guarantee of suffrage, the enactment of civil rights. Those efforts took years, decades and centuries before being actualized. The challenge for any disenfranchised people has always been to press the cause of their humanity, until the insistence of their value eclipses the injustice done to them.

That surpassing moment occurs, when enough people privileged by their enfranchisement gain the conversion of conscience to create it for others. That critical mass point occurred for the great campaigns mentioned above. When it becomes evident amongst the men of the NBA, women in the NBA will become a customary reality. Relative to gender equity, women must always campaign its validity, but it will require men to reconcile it amongst themselves for it to become a reality. A lesson from baseball demonstrates this.

Jackie Robinson is remembered for creating a seismic shift in America's race relations, by breaking the color barrier in baseball. While he did, in fact, create that shift, he didn't actually break the barrier. It is undeniable that Robinson, demonstrating heroic nobility, incomprehensible restraint and unimaginable courage triumphed over the blatant bigotry, the egregious indignities and the daily death threats that accompanied every moment of his playing against the white exclusivity of America's favorite pastime. Whatever praise has been lauded on him for his excellence as an athlete, an individual and an American are all warranted and deserving without stipulation. However, the disconcerting truth is there was nothing Robinson did or could do to autonomously and unilaterally effect his entry into Major League Baseball. More to the point, he was allowed in by the daring of Branch Rickey, owner of the Brooklyn Dodgers, who for reasons more financial than principled, created the opportunity for Robinson to enter the league. Subsequently, more white owners, managers, coaches, teammates, fans and journalists entered a nearly two-decade national conversation that led to a conversion of conscience, which became sweeping and permanent for the entire league.

Had the Milwaukee Bucks hired Becky Hammond, a similar momentous, historic society-changing opportunity would have been created for women. And like Josh Gibson, Satchel Paige, Oscar Charleston, Turkey Stearnes and Cool Papa Bell, other Negro League players who were as deserving if not more so than Robinson to have been granted an MLB opportunity, there is an around the corner, down the block, mile-long line of women who have been standing in front of, next to and behind Becky Hammond, women who are as capable and deserving of the opportunity to a take a seat on the sidelines and in the front offices of the NBA's 30 franchises.

What remains for this to be realized is determining the content for the conversation. There are three questions that can be asked, when considering it:

1. What is the functioning mindset needed?
2. Why hire women?
3. What are feasible solutions for immediate impact?

Mindset

When considering women, ethnic/race minorities and the LGBTQ community, the issue of inclusivity is dependent on the perspective towards diversity. If diversity is viewed only as an obligation, then there will always be a reluctance for, a resistance to and a resentment of it. It will be viewed as an unfounded request leveraged by an undeserving people for an unfair advantage, an infringement on a proprietary claim preordained by a preferred gender, race and sexuality.

Consequently, considering inclusivity will always be seen as a forced concession to an enforced compliance, rather than a willing ratification of the universal humanity of others. This is why laws have proven necessary to mandate and protect measures for the equitable treatment of people. When Martin Luther King, Jr. was asked how he felt about the passage of the Civil Rights Act of 1964, he responded, "Morality cannot be legislated, but behavior can be regulated. Judicial decrees may not change the heart, but they can restrain the heartless."

Morality resides in the conscience, and a conversion of conscience changes the heart. This is what is required to replace what is heartless with what is heartfelt. That replacement is not a submission to guilt-gorging sentimentality. What is heartfelt defines what is deeply believed. This means that not only is something done because it is legislated to be right, fair and just but that it is done because it is believed to be right, fair and just. When this is the thought directive, diversity is viewed as an opportunity, and can be resourced for a greater exchange of thoughts, ideas and experiences to be cultivated for a greater level of creativity, ingenuity and productivity.

This is not a tremendous mentality leap for the NBA. It's a mindset already in place, but one that needs to be made more universal in its application. Decades ago, the league proved itself willing to opportunistically capitalize on the diversity of player talent that existed in African American communities across the country. It has also done so throughout the world, globally mining exceptional talent for the ongoing excellence of the league. There are currently 108 international players from 42 countries, in the NBA.

Players play the game. They are, in essence, the product the NBA markets to the world. The player diversity initiatives of the league have given it the highest product quality, of any professional league, worldwide. As a result, the NBA enjoys a global fan base, and has become an extremely lucrative commercial, business and financial success. The Forbes 2019 valuation of NBA teams estimates that the average team is worth $1.9 billion, up 13% over last year and three times the value from five years ago. That's a staggering appreciation, from the $10,000 franchise fee owners paid to the start the league in 1946. Last year, each team received more than $110 million from shared revenues. Such is the profitability of diversity.

Reluctance, resistance and resentment also greeted player diversity initiatives, but try to imagine the NBA now without them being carried forth. As unimaginable as it was for some to favor the possibility of benefit from being more inclusive of minority players, it remains unimaginable for others to likewise do so from being more inclusive of women. The NBA can again carry forth. History will again be on its side.

The required participants for this conversation, the men of the NBA, will have to expand their mindset beyond player talent, to similarly benefit from the exceptional talent pool of women capable of enhancing the excellence of the league. The onus of adopting and implementing this mindset as policy and practice is weighted more on some than others. Players can offer vocal support of and draw media attention to the issue, to promote and drive the gender equity conversation for the league, as they have done for other timely, socially conscious issues. In fact, the players seem to be ahead of the other men of the league, as many have expressed no qualms about playing for a female head coach. Also, their lead by example hiring of Michele Roberts is concrete demonstration of what they believe. But players cannot directly act to make changes about more female representation in the league. They do not have rule changing power for league policies, or hiring authority for team coaches and personnel. Owners, presidents, general managers and head coaches do.

Women

When public schools were integrated by the 1954 Brown v. Board of Education decision, the courts differentiated between *de jure* segregation and *de facto* segregation. De jure means that it legally exists because laws mandate it. De facto means that it socially exists because of custom, habit and voluntary conduct. This differentiation is relevant to the NBA. There are no rules or by-laws that restrict or prohibit women from being head coaches or executives. However, there is a custom, habit and voluntary conduct that makes this a reality. When considering the outcome of the landmark Brown case, the choice between de jure gender exclusion and de facto gender exclusion can be thought of as either being unconstitutional or unconscionable.

A substantiated truth offered from history further underscores this. Nations that most severely repress and oppress entire segments of their populations lag behind technologically, economically, socially, culturally and politically than nations that don't. Why would governments, businesses, organizations and teams be an exception to this? The highest achievement of a people is more apt to be accomplished when its total population is tapped for ideas, talents and skills not when it is limited to the craft of a single gender, race or ideology. In America, women comprise 51% of the population. To think that the chiming of the bell, on America's finest hour, will only be rung by the hands of men is either a statistical absurdity or an obstinate irrationality, or both.

This absurdity-irrationality likewise confronts the NBA. Its men feel no motivation and operate with no mandate to meaningfully address the gender disparity of the league. It has been preferable and easier to consider this a gratuitous concern, or to impose arbitrary criteria for women that it does not impose for men (how many owners, presidents and general managers have played in the NBA?), or to dismiss women for not having the necessities (aptitude, organizational skills, temperament, etc.) or desire, something former General Manager of the Los Angeles Dodgers Al Campanis once opined, as the reason for the dearth of black managers in professional baseball. It is worth noting that Campanis was once a teammate and roommate with Jackie Robinson.

During an October 2017 interview on *The Ringer*, at minute 1:38, Bill Simmons asked Masai Ujiri for his best management advice. Initially stumped, Ujiri answered, "Be more passionate than ambitious." Simmons was impressed by the response but with more time to think, Ujiri continued, "Can I say another one which is very underrated? Hire women. I am not just saying it...There is something about them that brings us to a level that...we think better...where our egos start to get in crazy places...they are really, really good...very level headed...and they just have a good way... of putting things in perspective." Simmons replied "...the one thing I've learned is...diversity of who is around you...and not just like what people look like, male and female, but backgrounds...where do you come from and what did you learn and what do you bring to the table that I'm not getting from this person...".

Simmons agrees that diversity has value, but his response reveals a logic loophole that dodges diversity as an equal opportunity for all. White Americans, relative to race, and men, relative to gender, often engage in a whitewashing and manstaining of diversity. To paint a *variety* of backgrounds and experiences within a homogeneous class of people, as being morally equal to the socially uplifting contributions from the cultural acquirements and insights of a heterogeneous society, is a self-serving exemption for behaving with bias. It is the immunity of entitlement not the rectitude of enlightenment, a privileged appeasement of conscience not a profound conversion of it.

This loophole has thwarted inclusivity, since the birth of the nation. From the outset, the opportunity for women to participate in every social, financial and legislative process and institution was denied, and the opportunity for African

Americans to merely be regarded as human was chained in bondage. This "Founding Fathers" mindset has allowed white men to affirm actions that advance them, to the setback exclusion of others. That those men came and come from different parts of the country with different life experiences, regional backgrounds and cultural upbringings did and has done nothing to safeguard against the exclusion that enables their exclusivity. This loophole is used in legislative bodies, boardrooms and executive suites from coast to coast. It is an intentional negation that cannot be excused for its deceptive justification.

That negation is countered by a reason Ujiri endorses for hiring women, "...we think better." Academic research supports this is a legitimate phenomenon. Groups that include women have greater success with collaboration. In fact, groups that are at least 50% women have the best results. A possible reason for this is an area of performance women consistently demonstrate having an advantage over men. Soft skills.

Most people comprehend and give great value to hard skills. These are defined as the practical and technical abilities specific to each job. They are learned from formal education, tutorial instruction, standardized training and trade certifications. They can also be quantified, graded and ranked for the tangible evaluation of performance. Some examples are: typing, reading, software development, computer programming, baking, carpentry, chemical engineering, neurosurgery, physical therapy, accounting, analytics, passing, dribbling, shooting.

Conversely, soft skills are not as easily quantifiable and are generally more undervalued. They are attributes and qualities derived from emotional and social intelligence rather than academic or technical intelligence. Though they can be acquired, they are more likely to be intrinsic to the character and personality of the individual. They enable people to interact more effectively and collectively with others. Some examples are: active listening, conflict management, strategic thinking, multitasking, integrity, reciprocal communication, supportive leadership, problem solving, empathy, social fluency, rapport development, collaboration, team building, work ethic.

According to research by the Hay Group, women outperform men in all areas of soft skills other than emotional self-control, in which case they show equal results. This enhanced competency enables women to have more conscientious consideration for how decisions and actions impact others, rather than evaluate potential outcomes mainly according to self-interest. It commissions an awareness and responsiveness that promotes better teamwork, fruitful partnerships and contributions to the establishment of work cultures that promote, protect and preserve communal participation rather than rebuff, restrict and reject it. With soft skill proficiency, women more consistently project a positive outlook; influence and inspire unity; mentor and model cooperative conduct; and reduce and resolve the tensions and conflicts of organizational politics.

Solutions

The NBA can regard gender diversity, with the same moral imperative it shows for racial diversity. As chief administrator of the league's players and overseer for the concerns of its owners, Commissioner Adam Silver is suited to the times to do so. For example, he does not punitively sanction players for being outspoken about political and social issues, something the NFL does. When Los Angeles Clippers' owner Donald Sterling sparked a public relations crisis, Silver took immediate action an issued a lifetime ban of Sterling from the league. During his tenure, the NBA has also addressed, through public service announcements, significant issues like AIDS, gun violence, gay shaming, domestic violence and gender equity (#LeanInTogether). These campaigns have been guided by the President of Social Responsibility and Player Programs, Kathy Behrens.

The NBA has fully embraced the social media technology of the day. So, fans who value gender equity, women and men alike, can express their concerns to the Commissioner and the principal owners of each team, by forwarding suggestions and solutions. Here are a few reasonable, result-producing measures that can create a measurable difference:

Talk more.

Many basketball fans have experienced talking to someone, who is disinterested or disinclined about the sport. They not only don't appreciate your love of the game, but they don't possess the basketball IQ or vocabulary to comprehend or respond to your narrative about it.

A similar truth exists for team owners, presidents, general managers and players who have been disinterested and disinclined about women as head coaches and executives in the NBA. Silver can counter this with consistent messaging to increase the gender equity IQ and vocabulary, throughout the league and fan base. He can apply his views about women in the NBA, to any current topic he is addressing regarding the operations, personnel makeup and future enterprise of the league. Moreover, he can promote gender equity as being essential to enhancing the longevity, creativity, ingenuity, productivity, marketability and fan base of the league. To the last point, the diminishing incomes of the middle class marks a purchasing decline in a male consumer all sports have always relied on. The female market still has an enormous upside for cultivating.

The more said more often, the less stigma, taboo and resistance—three words 51% of the country no longer wants to determine their opportunities.

Deadline a goal.

Without a deadline, most objectives end up dead. Establish concrete goals to create gender equity and assign a target date for achieving them. For example, by September 2019:

In a sector in which most men are almost entirely segregated from senior women professionals, the exposure will serve to desensitize, educate and even surprise men about what professional women are like.

- Each team can hire at least two women assistant coaches, analytics staff, medical staff and scouting staff.

- Each team can interview at least 3 women candidates for any open position. In a sector in which most men are almost entirely segregated from senior women professionals, the exposure will serve to desensitize, educate and even surprise men about what professional women are like.

- Continue the Basketball Operations Associate Program with a more aggressive recruitment of women on college campuses and universities, and a more visible promotion of it via career venues and publications for women.

- Erase the pay disgrace. The average woman earns just 80.7 cents to the dollars of her male counterpart. For Kristi Toliver, it's less than 10 cents. During her offseason from the WNBA, she was hired as an assistant coach for the NBA's Washington Wizards. However, WNBA players are limited to earning just $50,000 from offseason work. So instead of getting $100,000 or more like male assistant coaches, Toliver was only paid $10,000. A discouraging, if not insulting sum and a pay slight that often sends WNBA players overseas in the offseason to play for more money, rather than rest their bodies, as NBA players do, or pursue post-playing career development in professional basketball. A similar restriction on NBA players is meaningless given the salary disparity is so astronomical. When women are hired as coaches and executives, pay them exactly what their male counterparts are paid. Gender equity should also mean earnings parity.

- Don't be the sports league of yesterday's mentality, be the league of today's reality. WNBA players find themselves in a similar situation to as the world champion U.S. Women's soccer team, when it comes to pay equity and working conditions. The soccer team is now suing the U.S. Soccer federation to resolve this. It's a tough sell on integrity to pay players of the WNBA and the U.S. Women's soccer forty cents or less on the dollar, to what their male counterparts are paid. Doing so puts them at greater risks for financial stress, mental and psychological fatigue, isolation from being forced to play in foreign countries with language and cultural barriers and away from family and loved ones, injuries, relationship hardships and shortened careers as athletes. If Silver is considering adding more capital resources to the NBA's G-League, seeing it as another basketball product to market, he can also encourage and prompt WNBA owners to do the same.

Connect the connections.

Become the source of referrals for women professionals. Invest time to identify and learn about who the current and emerging women leaders are in other sectors and industries. This will not only expand the pool of candidates for participation in the NBA, it will also create a resource for WNBA players and other female athletes to find mentors to develop their business IQ. This will also help develop the gender IQ of the men in the NBA, about the competency of women in leadership positions.

Spotlight and highlight.

Always invite women to participate on panels and in conferences that are about the NBA. To not do show puts the league's professed interest in gender equity at risk, for being seen as pretense not sincerity. If girls and young women don't see women on the stage, they won't have much hope of seeing themselves in the league.

The NBA is highly regarded as being the most progressive professional sports league in the country. As such, it is positioned to take the lead on making standard what is still regarded as an exception. Then, one day it might be NBA Commissioner Nneka Ogwumike awarding the Larry O'Brien trophy to the NBA campion. Ogwumike, NBA. That even sounds like poetic justice.

6 Personality Types
You Should Avoid At Work

Oprah Magazine 5/11/16

1. The Moles

Who they are:

> Mole colleagues hide when they feel insecure, allowing
> problems to become overwhelming. Reluctant and quick
> to embarrass, they are easily intimidated.

How to identify them:

> Look for these socially inept types eating alone at the
> cafeteria, sitting in the back of the room at the training
> and sneaking away early at office parties. They may seem
> laid-back when passing on opportunities for promotions,
> but they would rather languish in one position than extend

themselves to advance. They can appear easygoing when accepting blame for a missed deadline, but actually lack the courage to confront the true offender. Fearful of risk, failure and rejection, they will shun attention at any cost. The moment your project requires communicating with others, moles will flee from their responsibilities and disappear under the radar.

What to watch out for:

You might find the reclusive and pitiful nature of moles to elicit your compassion. But moles only know how to burrow down. Align yourself with them, and you will fall down the same career-isolation hole they dig for themselves.

How to protect yourself:

Don't waste time helping moles become less isolated. They don't want to be noticed, and will convert anything you say into self-loathing. Count on them only for routine work that can be completed without drawing attention from senior management, especially for tasks which they volunteer to do.

2. The Panhandlers

Who they are:

Panhandler colleagues walk the line between performing at their job and hunting for constant recognition. They are time-stealing attention seekers desperate for continuous praise.

How to identify them:

> You'll find these gregarious types carrying on loudly at happy hour. They are the sycophants tailgating anyone who will toss them morsels of attention.

What to watch out for:

> At first, we are pleased when we meet panhandlers, because they are willing to go out of their way to do something for us, to demonstrate their loyalty. But their loyalty shifts like a leaf in the wind. As soon as panhandlers find a better source of affirmation, they will kick you to the curb, even in the middle of an important deadline.

How to protect yourself:

> Realize that panhandlers focus on praise the way addicts focus on drugs. To keep them on task, refrain from giving them praise until the very end of an assignment or project. The moment you start doling out the compliments is the moment you'll lose their attention.

3. The Pretenders

Who they are:

> Pretender colleagues are the con men and women of the workplace. They may appear self-assured but forever worry about being discovered as frauds.

How to identify them:

Pretenders misrepresent, embellish and exaggerate, creating misunderstandings and false expectations all around them. They will even manufacture a crisis, just so they can save the day.

What to watch out for:

Ironically, pretenders are capable and likable when a project is in the planning stage. Then, the effort required at the execution stage triggers them to begin hyping themselves and their abilities up. They become an ongoing source of frustration, disseminating misinformation that throws everybody off course, leaving colleagues scratching their heads trying to discern the truth.

How to protect yourself:

Keep track of their fabrications and contradictions to avoid being snared by a web of deception. When challenged about their problematic conduct, pretenders will often humble themselves. But humility is only a temporary state for pretenders. Keep them focused on facts and concrete deliverables, and give them accolades only for successfully completing projects.

4. The Headliners

Who they are:

Headliner colleagues have egos that are guaranteed to aggravate. They are arrogant status seekers convinced that everyone envies them.

How to identify them:

> The headliners are always interrupting at meetings and hijacking conversations. They are defensive when receiving feedback, and only interested in conversations highlighting them.

What to watch out for:

> Headliners don't choose friends. They target people to exploit, people they believe can elevate their status. They are manipulators only interested in how you can service their ambition. Headliners will step on anyone to get ahead.

How to protect yourself:

> Manage your relationship with the headliner by saying no to most requests that are outside of your job description, and require that your generosity be reciprocated before you help with their next 'favor.' Once they realize that they cannot use you to get ahead, they will concentrate on distinguishing themselves technically, so they can boast about their contributions to the project.

5. The Directors

Who they are:

> Director colleagues are obsessed with control. They cannot handle uncertainty, and they want to design the outcome of everything.

How to identify them:

> Directors are more interested in being right than in doing the right thing. They cannot tolerate anyone disagreeing with them, which means they're constantly alienating people. They are also the most unlikely co-workers to ever say, "Thank you."

What to watch out for:

> Heads up! Directors become loose cannons when they lose control. They will rant, insult and intimidate to keep and regain control, even if it means being disliked and feared by their colleagues.

How to protect yourself:

> With directors, don't yield until you've reasoned to a middle ground. Be clear about what plans are non-negotiable and be mindful of their verbal drive-bys—and also always wear your psychic Kevlar.

6. The Conflict Junkies

Who they are:

> Conflict junkies are a combination of all the other types described, grafted into the most toxic and hostile contagion to ever poison the workplace. If Ebola was a personality type, it would be a conflict junkie.

How to identify them:

They are the pathological bullies who harass even the most well-intentioned staff; the combative co-workers everyone has a horror story about; the rebellious employees so caustic, they send their superiors into septic shock. They are completely resistant to civility.

What to watch out for:

Like moles, conflict junkies may initially appear submissive, but this is a ploy that lasts only until they have adjusted to a new situation. Like pretenders, once acclimated, they become agents of disruption. CJ's go beyond the tactics used by directors to gain control, pitting colleagues against one another, sabotaging projects, undermining their superiors, withholding information to create conflict and misrepresenting situations to HR. Like panhandlers and headliners, they will go out of their way to feed their egos. The difference? They act with no concern for consequence, even when it threatens their own careers.

How to protect yourself:

Handling conflict junkies is more than a one-person job. Take advantage of your organization's policies, regulations and stated values. Leverage all penalties available, even those that require legal action, if needed. Report their conduct to HR, and encourage others to do the same so that you can build a case for their termination. If they cannot conduct themselves rationally and respectfully, you should refuse to assist, comply with, respond to or even acknowledge them. If all else fails, consider asking to be reassigned or taking a new job.

The categories featured were adapted from the book, Water For The Soul, *with permission by the author, Michael Tyler.*

A Season Deferred

Medium 5/12/19

THE BOSTON CELTICS HAVE BEEN eliminated from this year's playoffs, by the "Fear the Deer" Milwaukee Bucks. The Celtics dismissal from postseason play cannot be regarded as an upset. The moment the seeding was set, their fate was destined for an insurmountable showdown with the Bucks. No one outside of the Celtics organization and fan base had any hope or expectation that Boston would prevail and advance to the Eastern Conference Final. They were outmatched, outplayed, outcoached and outmanned, particularly when considering the critical absence of Marcus Smart due to injury, at the start of the series.

An opponent's superiority and an injury depleted roster would absolve any team from the harsh summary of failure. However, given how poorly the Celtics underperformed in postseason, their elimination is only the borne fruit of how dysfunctional the team played all season. Last year, the Celtics were a game away from defeating the LeBron James led Cavaliers and playing in the championship final. Preseason predictions had them highly regarded, as a team to emerge from the East. The post mortem is now underway.

Two individuals have had the most fingers aimed at them, for the Celtics not living up to expectations and their level of talent: future Hall of Fame guard Kyrie Irving and Head Coach Brad Stevens. Regarding the latter, Stevens pointed himself out for blame, immediately following the playoff-ending 116–91 loss against the Bucks.

The start of the 2018–2019 season had great promise—on paper. Kyrie Irving, the undisputed star of the team, and Gordon Hayward, a Brad Stevens protégé tailor made for Celtic pride, were returning to the roster. Paper gets crumbled.

Sports media analysts and fan critics ironically blame the demise of the team on their return. One perspective sees it as the consequence of having a gluttony of riches. The Celtics' roster is so replete with talent, that finding a balance to direct an effort for a championship is too great a challenge for any coach or group of players. That a player as talented as Gordon Hayward struggled to find comfort, while players like Terry Rozier and Jaylen Brown struggled to find minutes supports that perspective. Likewise, the strategically agile Brad Stevens appeared flatfooted about the team's internal dynamics, which became more vexing when they became so publicly visible.

Most observers, however, lay the reason for the team's disappointing season at the fantastically talented and fleet feet of Kyrie. This perspective concludes that his me-centric, hero ball, shot clock consuming style of play proved too alienating and disruptive for a squad that found tremendous cohesion and success at the conclusion of last season. With his presence, the chemistry of the team no longer supplied the energizing elixir of splendid solidarity. It could only brew the toxic tincture of a debilitating discord.

Neither assessment is complete on its own. Combined, they draft a more comprehensive critique. A more complete evaluation could consider, that the genesis of the Celtics' calamity can be traced back to before the first jump ball of the regular season. The adage, failing to plan is planning to fail, offers a clue.

I had a concern about their talent riches, when I spoke with a principal of the franchise in early October 2017, just days before the start of the season. The conversation lasted 40 minutes. I proffered myself as a consultant for the organization, to aid in developing better leaders. My premise was that their talent abundance could put team unity at risk for destabilizing tensions, due to the significance, roles and minutes allocated to players. I suggested that preparation to address this concern would be required, to preempt that potential.

When I was questioned about the type of preparation I had in mind, I described grouping players into cohorts. The structure and activities of the cohorts would be designed to weave the fabric within each group with greater cohesion. This would provide a learned and shared framework for how players could collectively unify as a team.

I was challenged for details about activities and other ideas presented, which I furnished but my offer was eventually declined. It was explained to me that there was no way I would be granted access to the players. Accepting this, I offered to only advise the coaching staff about how to facilitate the player cohorts. Also declined. I was told, "Brad Stevens understands team basketball", and later in an email "Our coaches and players seem well connected".

I never questioned Brad Steven's aptitude. My perspective was more an understanding, that developing a cohesive team culture is quite different than expertly preparing a team to execute and play well. A failure to understand the former can prevent the latter. Not even the most sympathetic judgment could support that this season's Celtics exhibited a cohesive team culture.

The team was set to perform at a high level, when I had that October conversation. Moreover, Stevens had an impeccable record stemming from his Butler College coaching days. Even after having lost Hayward five minutes into the season, and

Irving with 17 games remaining in the season, the team looked ready to leverage its talents to conquer LeBron James, going into the playoffs in 2018. Extending the Cavaliers to a game seven in the series was a testament to that. The thunderous dunk by Jayson Tatum over LeBron was an emphatic declaration that they would not go gentle into the night. Despite the series loss, the Celtics left NBA fans and speculators very optimistic that the 2018–2019 season would be their year.

As a teen, when I watched Phil Jackson coach Michael Jordan and the Chicago Bulls to consecutive championships, I thought I was witnessing a new era of "basketball mindfulness", a process of harnessing the power of self-awareness for personal improvement. It never totally caught on. Any coach can pass out books, burn sage and integrate meditation as a practice. But what accounted for the domination the Bulls demonstrated, aside from Jordan's brilliance, was that Jackson's preparation created a near psychic connection between the players. They performed as if they were neuropathically linked. When they took the court, that connection gave the Bulls the singular focus and unified effort to do everything all the time, to win. For them, there was no such thing as home court. Every stadium and arena they entered was theirs and when they came to play you, they came to claim it. The onslaught was sublime.

This same approach to coaching ushered a Jackson disciple, Steve Kerr, to the Golden State Warriors. He immediately prioritized team unity and joy for the game. The result of this mindset preparation has fashioned what many other NBA teams still find elusive: an environment in which the staff and players can immediately address and move through challenges, in a manner that brings them closer together.

Several teams operate with a superstar player getting 30+ minutes of play, demanding the ball and directing the other players to stage his prominence for team success. The most extreme examples of this have been James Harden and Russell Westbrook. Kyrie Irving now ranks amongst them. But today's younger players have a different attitude towards that domineering license. They came up in an era that is less command-and-control and more rapid prototyping. They have been schooled on how to campaign and market their brand through social media. They don't view the old school ways of complete reverence and wholesale submission to a veteran hierarchy, as their way of seeing things. They aren't so amenable to the pecks of a pecking order.

Many Celtics players went on record this season, about the problems that plagued the team. Some felt relegated to being bit players, in a performance they had previously casted them in starring roles. Others grew disaffected and disillusioned about the lack of direction, cohesion and leadership of the team. A few players were cognizant early on of the potential hazards to their success but seemed hopeful victories would eliminate the threats. Winning often times cures what sickens a team.

Regardless of the cause of player dissatisfaction, a common concern surfaced. There appeared to be no recourse or solution to alter the circumstance. The team's presumed leader, self-absorbed with his exploits, and its head coach, confounded by the dramatic change with his team, were not able to course correct and navigate out of the whirlpool of their predicament. This led to a growing resignation about the season, that permeated through the team.

When Kyrie returned from his injury, his teammates were eager for and receptive to his leadership. They were certain that he was the key component, to advance them to a championship. They wanted him to level up *their* team, but for Kyrie that meant them playing on *his* team. Despite the prior year's success, Kyrie treated his fellow players like ancillaries there for whatever he wanted to happen on the court, not as valued contributors for a collaborative team achievement.

As the degree of alienation rose, Kyrie blamed other players, which created more alienation. Tensions came to a head in early March, when Kyrie aired comments that triggered reactions from several teammates. According to Kyrie, the resulting tumult was quickly resolved, on the March 4th cross-country plane ride to San Francisco. He told the media "That long plane ride helped us out". That improvement was short-lived. Kyrie, for all his talent, character and intelligence, lacked the self-awareness and self-analysis to assess the magnitude of the problem. What further complicated this was that no one, not even Brad Stevens, appeared willing or able to confront and convince him that his leadership meant him needing to change. He would have to become less me-centric and more we-centric, for the team to actualize its potential. To that point, there exist another wounding irony.

During a March 2018 *Work Life* podcast, Brad Stevens talks with host Adam Grant about his success as a college coach at Butler, practicing the 'Butler Way'. This is a culture set based on humility, passion, unity, servanthood and thankfulness. Brad explains to Adam that humility is about having "a commitment to something bigger than yourself", and that "it's easy to get caught up in yourself…as crippling as adversity can be, if you don't have humility, success can be just as crippling". The podcast relocates into the Butler gym, where the team practices in t-shirts that say, "Team above self". Adam goes on to narrate that "the goal of the Butler Way is to make sure players don't try to become individual stars than the bigger team". Then Stevens unwittingly drop his tell, "It's hard to put into words but you can feel it".

His difficulty putting it into words may have been his downfall this season. There is a linear progression between words, thoughts and actions. If you don't have the words, you can't conceive the thoughts. If you can't conceive the thoughts, you won't produce the actions. Game over.

If Brad had found the words, he might have more effectively addressed Kyrie about how his conduct was detrimental to the success of his team. He might have conveyed to the other players, that their roles were not to subsidize Kyrie's sense of entitlement and his narcissistic pursuit of glory. He might have facilitated a conversation for the entire team, to help express themselves with mutual support and constructive candor. He might have organized small player cohorts to strengthen the team's social fabric, for players to comfortably and regularly have open dialogues and preempt their problems. And on that magical plane ride from Boston to San Francisco in March, from which Kyrie emerged to tell the media that the team had made amends, Stevens just might have played, over the airplane speakers, the podcast in which he describes the Butler Way.

Players practice for hundreds, if not thousands of hours perfecting their shots, refining their footwork, improving their dribbling and sharpening their passing. They put themselves through arduous training to condition their bodies for the demands of a grueling season. The go through great lengths, to extract insights and knowledge from film sessions. They scrimmage more times than a season's 82 games, to polish the plays and schemes they must execute during the game. They impose a self-discipline on every aspect of their lives—what they eat, how they sleep, when they seek treatment.

They do all of this to prepare themselves for the job that is their passion, to play a game at a level most of us only achieve through fantasy. But that game is played between the ears, before it is played on the court. Their mental preparation for unbreakable unity, overcoming adversity, being immune to distractions and constructive leadership is as vital for their success, as all the physical preparation they undergo. Without it, they cannot maximize their talents, exceed expectations and realize their potential. Without it, all plans lead to failure.

Interview Techniques That Get Beyond Canned Responses

Alicia Bassuk/Jodi Glickman

Harvard Business Review 2/19/16

ACCORDING TO ELON MUSK, A good way to tell if a candidate is fibbing about his or her qualifications is whether they can use a personal story to illustrate a particularly telling experience. "If someone was really the person that solved a problem, they'll be able to answer the question on multiple levels," he says. "Anyone who really solves a problem never forgets it."

Whether it's because they're hiding something, or because they're just plain nervous, job candidates often offer canned responses. One option is to dismiss the person outright, but you may actually be missing out on a great candidate who's instinctively gravitating toward answers to questions they spent time preparing.

If you're willing to dig in, take a few risks, or change tactics, you can get a better sense of the real person behind the candidate, and to catch a glimpse of what it would be like to work together. After all, when you get someone to show vulnerability and share a personal challenge that took them outside of their comfort zone, you open up a whole new window into the person sitting across the table from you—or in the case of Musk, identify important warning signs.

Here are three ways to gain insight beyond the resume, beyond the prepared responses, beyond the typical, "tell me about a time you failed" questions.

Practice on-the-spot coaching. Let's assume you're interviewing Maria for a chief of staff position. Previously, Maria was a fundraiser for a non-profit. She is professional, articulate, sharp, and enthusiastic.

If Maria is answering your questions too succinctly and you'd like to hear more depth in her answers, give her a coaching directive:

> "Maria, can you please answer the same question by telling me a story with an arc?"

If Maria stumbles, or can't seem to answer a seemingly simple question, such as "Can you describe your leadership style?", give her a different coaching directive:

"Let's change the question. How would your staff describe your leadership style?"

By giving Maria some on the spot coaching, you can assess several character traits:

1. Does Maria understand the feedback? Does she "get it" quickly and is she able to take action and redirect in the moment?

2. Is she receptive to your feedback, or defensive?

3. Does she know how to ask clarifying questions?

4. Does she integrate the feedback into the rest of the interview—or does she continue to offer succinct answers or stories without an arc?

If your answer is "no" to any of the above questions, it may give you pause about giving Maria the thumbs up to head to the next round of interviews.

Interview candidates in a group. Southwest Airlines invites groups of people to interview for flight attendant positions at one time, largely to observe the social interactions among candidates during a naturally high-stress situation. Interviewers then ratchet up the stress level by cold-calling specific candidates to answer questions, and creating scenarios which strain social dynamics—such as giving candidates opportunities to prove themselves without throwing others under the bus.

The interviewers then sit back and watch the situation play out, getting answers to such questions as:

1. Who emerges as a natural leader, building on the strengths of others or changing the flow of dialogue for the better?

2. Who challenges and brings out the best in others?

3. Who personifies the spirit and culture of Southwest— taking their work, but not themselves, too seriously?

4. Did someone find a way to disagree without doing so at the expense of another candidate?

Conversely, those who are challenged by the collaboration will likely miss out on opportunities to add value to the conversation. They may contradict another candidate or isolate themselves from social interactions before or after the group interview.

Test the fit. Lastly, the interview is a perfect time to test the cultural fit of the candidate. Vosges, a company that sells artisan chocolates and that one of us has worked with, evokes a brand that is hip and creative. This leads some candidates to expect a flexible workplace (i.e. working from home) with little to no face-time. In fact, Vosges' culture is built on the energy that comes from all employees working in pods throughout the office, and meetings held in beautifully decorated rooms adjacent to the factory floor.

Asking people detailed questions about culture is an effective way to expose work preferences, assumptions, and biases.

When a candidate says they're looking for an entrepreneurial culture, ask them to define what that means, using stories from their past or specific examples about what they want in the future. Do they read "entrepreneurial" to mean a culture that allows employees to run their own group as an independent business, or does it signal a workspace with whiteboard walls and beanbag chairs? Is a culture with a strong sense of community one that offers a general sense of collegiality and group lunches, or one that encourages and creates opportunities for community service and social activities outside the office?

A similar thing happens at Coyote Logistics. Their head of marketing says the company give candidates a manual about its culture, and then ask them to articulate the ways in which it's fit for them—and ways in which they will enrich it if hired. They want to make sure candidates know what they are signing up for and that's good for both the company and the potential employee.

On the spot coaching, group interviewing, and cultural fit dialogue gives you more and better information about your candidates. It also insures that you'll find stronger employees whose skill sets and mission align with your organization because you've seen beyond the resume and beyond the prepared responses. You've both vetted one another on a deeper level—making for better hiring and happier employees in the long-run.

Tips For Leading An NBA Team

Medium 4/10/19

THE LOS ANGELES LAKERS SELECTED Lonzo Ball as the second player picked overall in the NBA Draft on June 22, 2017. Ball was touted as a redeemer of a Lakers franchise that had fallen from the glory of its past. That same day, the Lakers announced a trade to acquire the draft rights to Kyle Kuzma. One of the players jettisoned from the team was D'Angelo Russell, now the centerpiece player of the Brooklyn Nets.

The move was not entirely unexpected by Russell. He and Ball played the same position, and it had become clear that Ball would be given the ball the moment he shook Adam Silver's hand. What Russell could not have expected was the draft-day commentary by Magic Johnson. At the press conference introducing Ball, Johnson said of Russell, "He has the talent to be an All-Star. We want to thank him for what he did for us. But what I needed was a leader. I needed somebody also that can make the other players better, and also that players want to play with."

That devaluating comment has led to a great irony. After having his leadership and likeability questioned, if not disparaged, by a Lakers legend and leader of five championship teams, D'Angelo Russell has truly become what Magic Johnson opined he wasn't, by leading the once lowly Brooklyn Nets to the playoffs. He is also highly regarded by his teammates, his organization and his community. There is a karmic significance to this given that Magic Johnson has suddenly and surprisingly resigned as team president, and the Los Angeles Lakers will be watching the playoffs this year, instead of participating in them.

A key point of that irony is that in the summer of 2018, Russell reached out to the one player Johnson has positioned as the basketball messiah, who will lead the Lakers back to the promised land of banners, parades and rings—LeBron James. Seeking tips about leadership, Russell sought trophy-earned counsel from King James. LeBron told him, "You have to be prepared mentally to go out and dominate every game, and then your teammates will follow that." The advice has been well applied.

Subsequent to his trade and Johnson's comments, Russell displayed something that is a hallmark feature of leaders. In the era of social media, he could have easily publicly retaliated against Johnson and the Lakers, for the very public slight he received as a parting gift. Instead, Russell accepted his fate, welcomed his opportunity and moved on by taking the higher road to a more positive reaction. What he displayed by doing so is character. During a time when so many players are so preoccupied with their social media persona, a *Pulp Fiction* quote from Winston Wolfe underscores Russell's post-trade conduct: "Because you are a character doesn't mean you have character."

I have been a leadership designer for more than twenty years. A paramount truth about becoming a leader is that **leadership development is character development**. The growth, progress and achievement of the individual determine the growth, progress and achievement of the leader the individual can become.

Leadership development can take several weeks, months or even years but there are techniques that can be quickly learned and immediately applied. Here are some tips that D'Angelo Russell and every NBA player can use to improve their leadership ability.

Leadership Tip 1: Own Your Expectations

The phrase 'lead by example' is as often misunderstood, as it is essential. Beyond vein-popping training, mind-altering hours of drills and a sweat-soaked performance during the game, to lead by example means to never demand or require of anyone that which you are not willing and committed to

doing yourself. Whatever expectations you have of your teammates, coaches and franchise, first address and resolve it within
yourself. Accept responsibility for a continued duty to do this,
and engage a continuous conduct to help those around you
do the same. Owning your expectations means exactly this:
first become what you expect others to be.

Three ways to start:

1. As a leader, hold the moral and ethical compass for
    your teammates. Where they go will be influenced by
    where your conduct directs them. Learn, know, invest
    in, uphold and enforce the guiding principles and stan-
    dards of the franchise. These are the coordinates that
    map out the culture and identity of the organization.

    To think of it another way, your disposition to the
    principles and standards of the franchise directly affects
    the social health of the team. Indifference to or flouting
    of them becomes a virus of misconduct that rapidly
    spreads throughout the locker room. Immunize your
    team with your behavior. Be what protects them from
    being infected by conduct detrimental to the team.

2. Being a leader is not a self-absorbed title that only
    considers how others play a supporting role to the leader's
    stardom. Effective leadership comprehends that one
    has never beaten five, and that the drama of a winning
    performance depends on the entirety of the cast.

Seek to maximize the talents and contributions of everyone on the team. The unselfish support of those you share the floor with multiplies the effort of everyone. The team goal is the greater pursuit. If you think otherwise, find an individual sport to play.

Spend time helping each player expand their strengths and eliminate their weaknesses. Do this to earn their trust of your direction, judgment and confidence to achieve, especially in the most critical moments.

3. Cohesive invincibility is the primary focus of leadership. The strongest bonds create the most unyielding determination. The formation and fostering of the bonds between your teammates is your obligation.

As the principal mediator of disagreements and conflicts, initiate and participate in activities designed for team unity. Dissuade and disavow the public rebuke and ridicule of everyone on the team, by anyone on the team. Forge and safeguard the integrity of connections your teammates have to each other to build the highest level of fellowship.

Leadership Tip 2: Value Not Volume

Volume is not only measured by decibel levels of loudness, but also by frequency of occurrence and magnitude of amount. Constructive leadership is not about being the loudest voice, or the voice heard most often. It is about having a voice that others find value in listening to. The mvp (most vocal player) isn't always the MVP (most valuable player). Add value to how you communicate.

Preface your intent to speak by asking yourself one key question: Is what I'm about to say going to help or hurt my team? Answering that question is not only about what you say, but how you say it and to whom you say it to.

Three ways to start:

1. Less than 20% of what you communicate to others is what you actually say to them. More than 80% is conveyed nonverbally—tone, facial expression, body posture, hand gestures, eye contact. Become more aware by imagining the younger version of the player you are speaking to. This will temper the delivery so that it is more productive than problematic.

2. Civility is the lubrication of society. Those who fail to learn this are destined to produce friction. Friction can wear down and destroy the parts and gears of any machine. Your team is your machine.

   To protect it from friction, check the lubrication of your consideration when communicating with others. Is your manner of speaking yelling, hostile and demeaning or is it measured, empathetic and inspiring? Is it laced with obscenities and insults or is it guided by respect and encouragement?

Leadership is about reaching higher and rising to the next level. You cannot elevate if you denigrate. Also, people are more apt to value your leadership, when they feel you value them. Appreciation is often rewarded by dedication.

3. Just as all players have a shot pocket, every player has a "talk pocket", a preferred manner that enables their most comfortable and effective reception for advice, instructions, corrections and critiques.

    Players may share similar experiences and backgrounds, but they all have their own frames of reference and capabilities for interaction. By anticipating this mentality diversity, you are more responsive to it. If you want your teammates to score on being receptive to you, learn their pocket for processing what you say.

Leadership Tip 3: Take As Much As You Give

Often times, those in leadership positions acquire an authoritarian mindset. This way of thinking tends to be averse to accountability, chronically judgmental, needlessly confrontational and relentlessly overbearing. Nothing about this mindset, and the conduct it produces, will enable anyone to have the necessary ability for self-examination that the greatest leaders possess.

Submit yourself to the same scrutiny, assessment, feedback and critique you are in rank to give to others. Seek it out. The leader who is best listened to is the leader who learns to listen better.

Three ways to start:

1. Rather than exonerate yourself for bad conduct or absolve yourself of the negative impact your statements and behavior, apologize without reluctance or in exchange for acknowledgement or favorable concession.

2. Request feedback sessions with your teammates and coaches, during which you do the least amount of talking. Offer your comments as questions with an earnest curiosity and interest in hearing honest and unrestricted input.

3. Work independently with every teammate and find what each needs from you to play better with you, and to become a better player for the team. Take notes to signal your commitment, and incorporate what you learn into your approach to the game.

Interviews with players, coaches, general managers and team presidents often prompt comments about leadership. Sports analysts, commentators and journalist likewise touch on the topic. Unfortunately, too often 'leader' is used as a cliché term that labels a desirable character component, rather than discussed with any meaningful conveyance about what it really is. It's like being able to see a color, but not being able to describe it.

Being a team leader does not equate with being the leading scorer or the "face of the franchise". Some of the best leaders spend more time watching the game from the sidelines, than playing on the court. What does equate with being a leader is a fervent and genuine desire to help everyone better their best.

Teams will continue to demand this character component of their players, and players will remain eager to meet that demand. Every off-season provides an opportunity to acquire it. Every regular season provides the games to apply it. D'Angelo, you are well on your way.

3 Stand-Up-For-Yourself Strategies For Sensitive People

Oprah Magazine 6/08/17

EVER BEEN BASHED FOR WEARING your heart on your sleeve? Slammed for being thin-skinned? Knocked for not being able to take a joke? In a world filled with microaggressions and macro hostilities, psychic bruising is often difficult to avoid. But you don't have to see your sensitivity as a character flaw. It could indicate that you are accurately reacting to an antisocial allergen—in other words, *jerk pollen.*

Everyone has sensitivities. Some of us respond by striking back with anger and rage. Others bury, deflect or mask their reactions, fearing retaliation for any comeback. If you're sensitive, what can you do to handle those difficult moments? How can you cope?

Start by rethinking what it means to be "sensitive." After all, it's an ability to see, hear and feel the nuances of human experiences that don't register a blip on the radar screens of others. And as radar screens detect threats, hazards and anomalies, you likewise have a detection capacity for spiritual peril. So, when confronting an incoming threat or a situation where you might be hurt, start by taking these steps:

1. Be a "BITCH"

Rather than thinking of it as a misogynistic slight, embrace this word as an instructional acronym: Being In Total Control of Herself. If you sense a nano-vibe of incivility, set your compass for self-control with this one simple truth: When people drop depth charges on you, they reveal the content of their character, not the basis of your being.

As an executive coach, I tell sensitive clients to assess damage with a "sticks and stones" reality check: Are you bleeding? Have you lost consciousness? Did you lose a limb? No? Then you're still afloat.

2. Scan for Specifics

It's not easy to do in the moment, but it's imperative that you remind yourself that this isn't about you; it's about them. This allows you to assess your situation for factual information—the *exact* words and conduct of your offenders. Did he call you a name? Did she shout and curse? Did he pound the desk? Did she point her finger in your face?

3. Reword. Rethink. Respond.

Words form thoughts, and thoughts lead to actions. So, while, yes, you may feel "hurt", "helpless" and "humiliated," those words form thoughts that lead to passive actions. If you think of yourself in these terms, instead of standing up for yourself, you'll cower. Rather than hold your own, you'll yield. I advise clients to quickly remind themselves that they own their mental geography. Let no one invade your space. Your new words: "reject", "resist" and "resolve."

Next, shift your outer dialogue. When faced with a particular insult, you have to respond. Here's how: Without name-calling, strike at the insecurities their comments have revealed. A colleague and I have been using the line, "Your comment reveals much more about you than it does about me." But clients have told me that this might feel too aggressive in their workplaces, so I would advise variations, saying something like, "That's revealing how polarizing this topic is," or "Your comment is surfacing a significant rift." This type of comment allows you to defuse the current situation, protect yourself and make them think twice about returning fire.

What Women Put Up With That Men Don't

Oprah Magazine 2/08/17

LAST NIGHT, MY FRIEND EUGENIA and I went to a restaurant and took seats at the corner of the bar. An hour later, a man obviously who had been drinking nearly bumped into me. I reacted by holding my hands up, bracing for contact. He stopped directly behind my stool, brushing against it with his torso, as he began hovering over me.

I politely asked him to step back from my chair, telling him he was too close. Rather than comply, he stood there, leaning in with a drunken stare. Standing at least 6'2" with a wide, heavy frame, he was intimidating. With more insistence, I said, "You're in my space. If you don't take a step back, I'm going to scream." He moved closer, inches from face, quickly becoming aggressive and responded, "No, you're in my space."

Eugenia intervened with a courteous tone, also asking him to step back. He didn't.

Before last night, I would have cowered and yielded by moving to another area of the restaurant. I might have even left. But earlier in the day, I attended the Women's March on Chicago. I left with a mind shift that finally synchronized with something I had been told once, ironically by a man: "Your mind and your body are your real estate. Don't let anyone stake a claim on your property." He also told me that whatever land I was standing on was mine.

So, there I was, standing on "my land" in that bar, resenting the feeling that I had to make an accommodation for this jerk's behavior. I called loudly for the bartender to intercede. The man still refused to move. Other patrons, men and women, witnessed the situation but with no motivation beyond gawking. I faced the man and didn't move. I was committed to getting him off my land.

The bartender came and coaxed him away. I thought *away* would be out the door. Instead, the man was allowed to move across the bar, where he sat hunched over, glowering at me. I was not at ease, feeling at any moment he would return with more threatening intentions. I asked for the manager. When he came, I explained what had taken place, and what remained unresolved. I went on to say that this situation happens to many women, and that I found it unfair that I (we) have to move or leave to escape feeling uncomfortable, harassed and intimidated. I insisted that the man be made to leave, and that is exactly what he was made to do.

The situation was surreal. The moment I committed to standing up to him, my courage kicked in. Why? Because courage is the ability to act when confronted with fear. Interestingly enough, you have to do the very thing you're afraid of to get it.

As I watched the man walk out the door, I realized I had finally done it. I *flexed*. My fiancé gifted this word to me when I was frustrated from being too slow to respond to a rude remark. He believes that to "flex" means to confirm your self-worth by defining it at all times, and defending it at a moment's notice. And that the first step is to state your most simple truth the moment you are aware of it.

Earlier that day, I had watched more than 200,000 women flex on the streets of my city, women who had refused to yield to the push of intimidation, the shove of bias and the slam of disparagement. Like them, we must all begin to flex, to define and defend our space. And we need to actively support each other, whether we know one another or not, when antagonizing situations occur.

Time to *flex*.

Leadership Crisis/
Crisis Leadership

HuffPost 10/12/17

T HE WORLD ECONOMIC FORUM'S 2015 Survey on the Global Agenda revealed that 86% of respondents perceive a global crisis in leadership. The survey assessed the general concerns and issues about leadership, not the specific issue of leadership during a crisis. That deficiency is more disconcerting in the face of increasing global social, political and economic complexities.

Donald Trump's presidency has been described, by pundits and politicians at every gradation of the political spectrum, as being in a state of crisis. With an approval rating as low as 38.8% at one point (Gallup Poll, July 2017), many Americans share the same perspective. The investigation into Russian involvement in the presidential election is a Watergate level risk, to the stability of his administration. The escalating nuclear provocation from North Korea, pushing nations closer to the brink of catastrophic conflict, poses his greatest foreign policy challenge. Epic hurricanes, exacting with deadly, destructive and decimating force have become his spotlight test for a national emergency. The virulence of America's racial virus, now disseminating at epidemic pace by those who perceive agency and alliance from the White House, is his contagion to remedy for national unity. Millions of Americans are facing the prospect of financial and physical ruination, as they stand in the crosshairs of his political reprisal targeting the Affordable Care Act. ISIS is still menacing, global warming is still threatening, immigration reform is still conflagrating, and Trump is still tweeting.

Each of these circumstances is an example of a crisis—a moment or situation of extreme dilemma, danger or disaster that requires complex, critical decision-making for resolution. Troubling to many people, across the country and around the world, is that President Trump acts more as Crisis-in-Chief, than Commander-in-Chief, creating or exacerbating such moments and situations almost daily. His temperament and conduct are causation for his crisis of leadership, which compound the very real and consequential crises that confront his judgment and the nation. Rather than respond and react with the critical thinking required of urgent stewardship that coalesces efforts and intentions, Trump's petty, petulant, impulsive and inflammatory inclinations are Balkanizing his party, his country and the international community with perilous potential.

Political and business leaders, regardless of party affiliation, have a moral, ethical and yes, patriotic responsibility to challenge, counter and if need be contravene Trump's direction of the nation's affairs and fate. To do so will require courage and resolve to act with a collaborative civic motivation for the welfare and preservation of our form of government, and the people it has been chosen to represent. Even more, it will require what Trump seems to be either completely averse to or completely void of—principle.

Principles are both the magnetizing elements and windrose that direct and display our moral and behavioral compass. They are conduct guides based on fundamental truths or foundational propositions. Leadership is dependent upon them because leadership provides direction. The ability to do so is not only evidence of character; it is also proof of adherence to principles. Without principles, direction becomes a perilous, heedless course.

When evaluating the character and leadership conduct displayed by President Trump, there appears to be no directional alignment to any fundamental truth or foundational proposition. Now our country is set for a course of heedless direction, on a path strewn with one crisis after another, some manufactured by President Trump and others the providence of forces beyond his control.

Are there guiding principles for leadership, in a crisis? Yes, but to understand and utilize them requires knowing and identifying the phases of a crisis:

1. **The event threat**: the actual cause and circumstance that is creating the extreme dilemma, danger or disaster.

2. **The rate of manifestation**: the amount of time, sudden v. slow, it takes for the threat event to become actual.

3. **The factor of realization**: the speed of awareness of the threat event—surprise v. gradual.

4. **The recognition-reaction interval**: the duration between crisis awareness and action for resolution.

Leadership is behavior, so the principles for crisis leadership are behavioral guides to adhere to, during every phase of a crisis. They are not step-by-step instructions for crisis management, the specifics of which vary by crisis type. For example, steps taken to address the public relations crisis following the BP Deepwater Horizon oil spill disaster differed from the response to the national security crisis created, when commercial airplanes unexpectedly flew into the World Trade Center. Instead, the principles listed below are philosophical guides (e.g.: The Golden Rule, noblesse oblige), that redefine the word "crisis" as a thought process for leadership conduct.

1. Composure sees through chaos.

Demeanor and decisions are hallmark and legacy of leadership in crisis, and the first has direct bearing on the second. Both are served well by calm. How you present yourself, to those who must execute your decisions, immediately imprints their organizational and administrative focus, resolve and implementation. How and what you decide as an action-response will reveal the aptitude and attitude of your judgment. Astute analysis and assessment require clarity, which comes when settling the dust storm of thoughts and emotions whipped up by the event threat. To do this:

- Know that you don't know everything, and that you are not expected to. This applies to the real-time dynamics and resolution know-how of the threat event. Direct your mental effort towards acquiring information, familiarizing yourself with the expertise of your personnel and establishing open, frequent and shared communication between all parties involved.

- Dissect the crisis into impact components that will allow you and your team to parcel out the complex task of resolution according to departmental specialization, for a more rapid and effective response.

- Resource your team with all that is required for them to execute your decisions. This will give you confidence that you are optimizing the response potential, while assuring your team they are fully supported.

- Keep your messaging positive. Negativity feeds stress and fuels panic. Judgment is established by analyzing and never proven by criticizing. Your words and conduct must be evaluative, encouraging and empowering.

2. Reliability means accountability.

Harry S. Truman became the 33rd President of the United States, assuming office after the death of Franklin D. Roosevelt. His most pressing order of business was ending the global crisis that was World War II. A sign on his desk declared the guiding principle of his leadership: "The buck stops here." He understood that responsibility for decisions made by him and his administration was his to personally acknowledge and accept, as a condition for holding office. This speaks to leadership accountability, the importance of which goes well beyond honorable conduct.

The ability to confront, manage, overcome and flourish beyond a crisis depends enormously on the single most sustaining aspect of human resolve, *hope—the emotional alignment to possibility.* When people cannot see or envision any possibility out of catastrophic circumstance, perilous predicament or an oppressive existence they will become hopeless. That mental state is the single greatest impairment of the human spirit. Without resolve, there is no resolution for any crisis.

The possibility of overcoming a dilemma, danger or disaster is the end-game focus of a crisis. A leader must inspire others to believe that possibility is a reality in progress. The effectiveness of a leader's inspiration is directly related to the degree of trust she/he conditions with others. Trust, in action, is the dependability of words and actions—*reliability*. Being answerable to the outcomes of your words, decisions and actions is *your obligation* to those who must carry out your orders of execution. The conviction of your obligation measures the integrity of your character, and your character determines the degree of trust you earn.

Your failure to achieve trust and demonstrate reliability will risk undermining the confidence, motivation and cooperation of everyone you administer with a fallout culture of resentment, dissension and blame. To safeguard against this:

- Communicate clearly, convincingly and consistently.
- Act responsibly, committedly and truthfully.
- Support openly, earnestly and continuously.

3. Insight is foresight.

Time is the most critical resource during a crisis. Lives, fortunes and fate can be lost if it is not maximized. Reactive thinking occurs after an incident and indicates time passed. Proactive thinking occurs before an incident and anticipates time to come. In other words, in a crisis, if you're not ahead, you're already behind.

Anticipate and plan for worst case scenarios, potential events, and unseen probabilities. This will require *insight*—the discernment of underlying truths and realities, in order to enable *foresight*—a precautionary view of the future.

Insight is informed by experience and perspective. The more varied those sources are, the more discerning yours will be. Enlist people with different knowledge, concerns and viewpoints. Pool their collective scope, develop protocols for what will and could happen, and improve existing protocols to streamline execution for the most rapid response achievable.

This process was engaged by John F. Kennedy, during the Cuban Missile Crisis. A year and a half earlier, he suffered the most disastrous foreign policy decision he ever made, the Bay of Pigs invasion. So, when Soviet nuclear missiles were discovered 90 miles from the U.S. mainland, he tried a different approach. Seeking to avoid the groupthink that undermined his decision making during the Bay of Pigs invasion, Kennedy ignored his military brass, who urged a military strike. With the fate of the planet and lives of 200 million at stake, a wrong decision meant a nuclear holocaust. Kennedy wanted a diplomatic resolution. He implemented a four-step approach, to come to his decision:

Step 1

Every member of the primary strategy team would function as a "skeptical generalist", approaching the crisis holistically rather than subjectively from departmental perspectives.

Step 2

Meetings were convened away from the White House, in informal settings.

This eliminated the turf-battles and conversational impediments of official titles and ranks, and allowed for more unrestrained discourse.

Step 3

The primary strategy team was instructed to occasionally meet without the President, to safeguard against restricting solutions to his viewpoints. Kennedy, like Lincoln, believed that diverse views, candid debate, exhaustive examination and dissent were vital to critical evaluation.

Step 4

The primary strategy team would then divide into sub-groups that would each develop alternative solutions. The sub-groups would then reassemble and debate the attributes of each solution, and let the best plan emerge on its merits.

This four-step approach still serves the presidential decision-making process. It is also taught in universities and business schools across the country, as the gold standard for executive decision making. More simply stated:

1. **Zoom out**—Expand the view off assessment beyond the narrow focus of occupational expertise.

2. **Liberate the debate**—For more constructive collaboration, free discussions from the restrictive formality of pecking orders and protocols.

3. **D.I.Y.**—Do it yourselves. Members of the decision-making team should meet without the chair in attendance, to insure a more objective, innovative, uninhibited evaluation for solution.

4. **Pick and choose**—Within the decision-making team, action groups should form and develop multiple solutions, then present and challenge them to determine the best plan of action.

4. Solidarity beats a common threat.

Everyone called upon to address a crisis is instantly impacted by it. Effective response requires the most devoted and diligent scale of teamwork attainable. Everyone must be fully informed of the objectives sought; thoroughly convinced of the plan and procedures drafted; and completely committed to a task performance that not only achieves goals but supports everyone else in achieving theirs.

Recognize that as a leader, the people around you, from department heads to entry-level staffers, from established veterans to unproven trainees, are all your partners. To view them merely as assets or resources diminishes the value of their contributions, the dignity of their dedication and the worth of their humanity. Do this and you will become desensitized to the mental, physical, psychological and emotional toll the crisis is exacting on them personally. You will also become indifferent to the exhaustive, self-sacrificing efforts they are making at your behest. This will prove alienating and disruptive to the crisis response.

Empathize and you will energize. Interact with your partners, at all organizational levels, and you will:

- Solidify their loyalty with face-time appreciation.
- Personalize their value with eye-to-eye recognition.
- Assure them of your support with handshake confirmation.
- Fortify their bond with huddle-up cooperation.

Maintain transparency to shore up their trust. Keep open lines of communication to incorporate their feedback. Assess their condition to prove your concern. If people know you have a genuine interest in their existence, and a general regard for their well-being they will deliver tirelessly, together. And only together will everyone prevail against the crisis.

5. Insist from yourself what you ask of others.

Hypocrisy is a derelict duty to and a fraudulent assertion of principles. It undermines every institution, every organization and every enterprise. For the leader who exhibits it, hypocrisy will likewise undermine his/her leadership, and everyone under it.

Integrity is an authentic adherence to and avid application of principles. It strengthens every institution, every organization and every enterprise. For the leader who demonstrates it, integrity will likewise bolster her/his leadership, and everyone under it. This is the inherent meaning in "Talk the talk, walk the walk." As a leader, particularly during a crisis, you must do as you speak.

Your words must have a single standard of judgment and a believability of purpose. Your decisions must address problems, without violating the rights and principles of the people executing and affected by them. Your actions will bear direct evidence of your character, beliefs, morals and ethics and when compared and contrasted to your words and decisions, that evidence will convict you of duplicity, or commend you as worthy of being followed. The importance of this will be evidenced by the performance of all you lead. If they do not believe in you, they will not believe in your professed regard for them, or what you ask them to do. Nothing will guarantee the failure of your leadership, and of the efforts you direct, more than this. In the words of Eleanor Roosevelt, "It is not fair to ask of others what you are not willing to do yourself.

6. Success is not an option, when it is a need.

When "must do", "will do" and "make do" all mean the same thing, then failure is unthinkable. Were this not the thinking of Abraham Lincoln, the Union would have not survived. And had not Franklin Roosevelt thought the same, The Great Depression might have been our great end. When survivability is not an alternative, success is an imperative. ·

Resolving a crisis is a "must do" situation. This is the over-riding task of leadership, in times of crisis. The resolve of one can be the will of many. A leader must embody and exemplify a resolve that galvanizes the "will do" effort of others, for a "make do" on their success.

If your primary mission is to "be right", then your hubris will do wrong by the goal required, the backup of those you are counting on, and the comeback of everyone counting on you.

If your greater objective is to receive tributes and praise, you will run an even greater risk of failing, and being criticized and condemned for a pompous disregard for the safety, well-being and lives of others.

Casualties, whether measured in property, belongings or lives are consequence to crisis. Every measure should be taken to minimize them. Don't incur the debt of conscience, for the incalculable cost of invaluable losses that could have been avoided. When you have no choice but to succeed, eliminate all reasons to fail. In the aftermath of a crisis, how well you will be remembered will be determined by how well you led.

"The Contender", starring Jeff Bridges and Joan Allen, was a movie about a political crisis looming over the White House. President Jackson Evans (Bridges) and Senator Laine Hanson (Allen) prevailed because of her stated conviction to a standard of conduct:

"Principles only mean something when they're not easy to stand by."

That quote stands stronger in reality as a guide for behavior, than as moral idealism in fiction. Its verity is also echoed in history by the words of Thomas Jefferson:

"In matters of style, swim with the current; in matters of principle, stand like a rock."

How About Some Quarrel
With Your Quail?

HuffPost 11/23/16

IT'S THAT TIME OF YEAR for festive family gatherings and holiday work functions. Pass the stuffing and gravy, serve up heaping helpings of gratitude and handout a grab bag full of gripes. Seasonal soirees bring people together, and with them differing opinions, perspectives and attitudes that can make for gift-wrapped difficulties.

Take the recent election, for example, which evidenced a country evenly split and equally disapproving. No doubt you have a mother, father, sister, brother, aunt, uncle, nephew, neighbor, cousin or coworker who voted for someone you didn't. Secret Santa? Yeah, right.

Family feuds and office arguments are as common to seasonal celebrations as ugly sweaters and overcooked turkey. One grudge, one insult or one too many sips of mulled wine can take the fire out the fire place and set a gala ablaze. So, take more than macaroni to your next potluck party. Bring some *mental bitters* to help digest any disagreements.

Decorate Your Spirit

Before attending or hosting a gathering, give yourself a gift—some peace of mind for the piece of mind you're willing to give to the occasion. Decide that you are not going to be triggered by anyone or drawn into any night-ending drama—no matter who, no matter what, no matter why. Festoon your mind with grace and goodwill, friendship and fun. Sidestep, segue, nod and non-sequitur your intention, to jingle your bells past wind-chilled comments and grouchy grinches.

Make Your Own Snow Globe

Imagine having a winter wonderland in a bubble and it's all yours, inside your mind. The world inside your head is what you make it, so seal off your conscious thoughts from negativity. Keep all instigators outside your emotional dome. Don't let anyone shake you into a flurried state. Keep the atmosphere inside your figurine serene. You control it.

Smile Through It

Act the way you want to feel, and soon you will feel the way you act. There's science behind it. It takes 5 pairs of muscles (10 in total) to simply turn up the corners of your mouth; 3 pairs of muscles (6 in total) to turn down the corners of your mouth. Smiling is a better workout for your face than frowning. Also, smiling, like breathing and laughing, activates the release of mood-altering hormones and neurotransmitters that enhance your state of mind. Buddhists practice this, which is why in all statues you see, Buddha is getting his smile on.

Go For Dessert

Some topics of conversation are highly prone to controversy and dispute: politics, religion, race, family secrets, caloric consumption. When you find yourself on the peripheral or in the midst of a contentious exchange, get some pie:

Put some distance between you and the conversation.

Invite others to join you for a more mutually entertaining and less joy draining discussion.

Embrace the once a year opportunity to voice the call for harmony, to silence the clamor of conflict.

Dish Out Diplomacy

Not all spirited conversations are destined for a dispiriting end. If you find that you are enjoying a stimulating and challenging bout of words, be mindful to serve with respect, dole out with discretion and carve with civility.

For Women, What's In a Name?

HuffPost 11/18/17

L AST MONTH MARKED THE 26TH Anniversary of Anita Hill's testimony against Clarence Thomas. As a college student at Wesleyan in 1991, I was gripped by the gravity of the moment: the confirmation hearing for a Supreme Court Justice nominee, conducted by an all-white male, fourteen-member Senate Judiciary Committee, brought to a tipping point by the accusations of a lone, African American female.

I was awed by Hill's willingness to step from behind the silencing curtain of victimization, to stand at the center-stage of history, under the intense spotlight of public scrutiny. Hers was a composure and courage millions of women still find impossible to muster. While viewing the hearing, I recalled how four years earlier, as a sixteen-year old, I was told by a restaurant owner that he would only give me a job as a waitress, if I promised to wear miniskirts. At that moment, I promised instead to never have a boss, so that no one could have that type of economically coercive, insulting power over me. I started a company at age 21, and 25 years later I am still my own boss.

So, when I watched the November 7th CNN Town Hall— Tipping Point: Sexual Harassment in America, featuring Anita Hill, I experienced a range of emotions I imagine other women felt while viewing it: self-affirming pride, empathy, sympathy and outrage—particularly as I learned of the hush-fund practice, financed by taxpayer dollars, used by congressmen and senators to silence women (and men) who have accused them of sexual harassment.

We are now in the midst of the #MeToo awakening, an awareness which left me feeling another emotion while watching that televised town hall—speculative disappointment. I say speculative because I watched wondering if Anita Hill, as I did, had an anticipation or expectation that the event would be a break-out conversation designed to forward-calibrate the status of women worldwide.

Instead, I saw a foot-dragging, sleepy dialogue that didn't come close to matching Hill's courageous confrontation of her harasser, from decades ago. To her credit, CNN anchor Alisyn Camerota moderated the event purposefully, adroitly and substantively. And to their credit, Hill's co-guests conveyed dismay and outrage about the poor conduct of the men who had harassed and assaulted them. Their narratives were poignant and arresting, as they recounted the tactless, intimidating and aberrant behavior of men they had worked with. But still, they fell short of fully using their voices. They did not name names.

Former Congresswoman Mary Bono said, "The reason that I don't [name him] is because he stopped. And I wouldn't say that if he didn't, but he did. And so, when somebody changes their way, they should be thanked." Bono protected the male colleague who had demeaned her with concealment, knowing only that he stopped his demeaning conduct with her. But what of the possibility that he continued demeaning other women?

Her exonerating grant of gratitude, recommending that men who stop their poor conduct be thanked, struck me more as Stockholm Syndrome appeasement than as a redemptive reward for character metamorphosis. If Bono's colleague had slapped her across the face, then stopped when she requested he do so, would she also keep him unnamed? Would she thank him? That her comments didn't trigger a jaw-dropping response, from any of the women onscreen during the broadcast, speaks to how pervasive a reality for countless women is the conduct of harassment—and appeasement.

Similarly protecting of a male colleague behaving with impropriety, Senator Kirsten Gillibrand stated, "I was grabbed by the waist, just with one hand, gently. And the gentleman said: Don't lose too much weight. I like my girls chubby." I'm aware of the customary protocol of civility amongst congressional and senatorial colleagues, to refer to each other as "gentleman" and "gentlewoman". But when a man disqualifies himself from such polite, well-mannered and honorable distinction, he should not be referenced as such. The waist-grabbing vulture of the voluptuous Gillibrand gave account to, also continues to circle the skies of inappropriate conduct, protected by the license of anonymity, free to lower his character and grip to pigeon other women, who must move around him in watchful discomfort.

The unwillingness of women to name their offenders is a conduct conditioned by a code of silence millions of women consent to and uphold, for many women share victim status inflicted upon them by the same perpetrator. This goes beyond the silencing culture of coercion men have created through punitive retaliations, rigged arbitrations, gag-order settlements and career-ending collusion. I am talking about the self-muting done by so many women who have suffered and endured the indignities of men, because they have given a greater priority to the reputation of men (good name, career impact, financial viability) than to the self-proprietorship of their own being.

I state this with full knowledge of and appreciation for the economic bullying, emotional duress, psychological manipulation, physical fear, subjugating threats and real danger many women live with because of sexual harassment. But I also wish to address this muting with the full awareness and intent of a personal audit that many, many more women face harassment without the response-negating consequences I just cited. We are a majority who can react and respond without concerns for financial retaliation, job security and physical reprisal. We are the magnifying multitude who can help the helpless amongst us to speak out against the transgressions and violations committed against them. We must voice the voiceless.

I can't think of a circumstance or situation when a code of silence is invoked and adhered to, for any reason other than to conceal misconduct and criminality. That concealment is generally orchestrated by the individuals guilty of misconduct and criminality, to protect themselves from exposure and prosecution. This is not the case with the accessory conduct I'm drawing attention to. When women invoke a code of silence, it is done to excuse the inexcusable excuses of the very men who have demonstrated misconduct and criminality towards us.

Our code of silence has a dual component. Both parts insure that we will continue to experience a disastrous dual consequence:

1. The perpetuation of a self-negating behavior we instruct to our daughters, granddaughters, nieces, cousins, students and co-workers. This lives on as an insidious indoctrination that makes us reluctant to defend ourselves. It also leaves us feeling overly concerned about appearing to be overly sensitive to tasteless, tactless comments and assaulting, abusive conduct.

2. It creates a 24/7 mental state of apprehension and fear we accept as our "normal". This is an exhausting, derailing preoccupation that continues to sidetrack our greatest abilities, aspirations and achievements.

Part one is our refusal to personally, directly and immediately address inappropriate behavior, or to report it to management or law enforcement. To overcome it, we must summon the courage to do so. But to do so, we must first understand the meaning of "courage"—having the ability to act when confronted with fear. We must also understand that the only way to get that courage we so sorely need is to do the very thing we're afraid of doing—holding men accountable.

One way to enable and empower yourself to act against inappropriate and egregious conduct is to become a flex practitioner. This means having an understanding of that word, as an application of conduct. Simply put, to "flex" means to define your value at all times, and defend it at a moment's notice. To become a practitioner means you will instruct your daily conduct to live this definition as your reality. It also means that you will commit yourself to sharing this definition and pledge of conduct, with as many women as you can, particularly when mentoring opportunities present themselves. We must create a "flex generation".

Part two is our unwillingness to identify the perpetrators of sexual harassment, and to call them out—**to name them**. This gives men the culprit shield that allows them to continue their harassment with impunity. The unwillingness of women to name names, and shine a protective light on predatory darkness, is not a matter of complicity or codependency. It is a matter of default participation in the creation of more victims. For every man we provide anonymity to, there exist a multiple factor of women he goes on to damage and demean.

Our cooperative silence, versus the coercive silence we must aid to overcome, is not unlike the code of silence of that infects police departments. Over the last year I have been in conversation with the Superintendent of the Chicago Police Department. Superintendent Eddie Johnson knows he must destroy the officers' code of silence, which keeps hush about departmental misconduct, if he is going to improve the relationship between officers and residents in the neighborhoods they patrol, especially low-income, real-estate distressed, minority communities.

Ironically, many residents of those same communities enact a code of silence that covers for criminals, out of fear of retaliation and distrust of the police. In both cases, the derelict population of individuals involved in wrongdoing is dwarfed by those who are not. The ratio of good cops to bad cops skews tremendously towards the good. Likewise, the communities skew towards law-abiding residents. Yet the felonious power that derelict population wields, and the detriment it exacts continues to affect the majority population who is silent to expose it.

Similarly, the majority of men conduct themselves with a non-threatening, non-harassing, non-insulting comportment. But when that majority of men remain silent about countering and calling out those men who behave to the contrary, the "department" of all men gets stigmatized. Likewise, when the majority of women remain silent about countering and calling out men who harass them, the "neighborhood" of all women lives under siege. And when we remain silent, we facilitate the victimization of other women, who must then live with the degrading and often times traumatizing impact for the remainder of their lives.

More, if not all women must become active participants, in advancing the legacy of Anita Hill's self-defining courage. We are now witnessing and bearing testament, to the efficacy and effectiveness of ending our code of silence. We need to further that effort by taking the next and needed steps to make #MeToo, #MeNoMore. Names like "Bill Cosby", "Harvey Weinstein", "Casey Affleck", "Bill O'Reilly", "Roger Ailes", "Roy Price", "Chris Savino", "Hamilton Fish", "Leon Wieseltier", "Michael Oreskes", "John Besh", "Louis C.K." "Roy Moore" and "Donald Trump" are all tumbling down the avalanche of accountability—because they got named.

The magnifying multitude of women I characterized earlier can do this. We are of position, capability, intelligence, self-preservation and coalition to do so. We only need the convincing will that will produce convincing change.

Our will needs to embrace the self-accountability, for flexing the reality we still only dream of, and it must constantly, conscientiously and collectively commit to standing with, for and behind each other against harassment, especially for those of us truly subjugated by circumstance. This support even includes reclaiming our physical space, something as powerful and enforceful as naming names.

Last weekend my friend Dana, a powerful executive and mother of four sons, was reading her iPad at a bar, inside a restaurant. Three drunk men, sitting very close to her, were talking loudly and directing sexually loaded comments at her. She told them to stop talking to her. They responded defensively, asking her why she was getting so angry, when they were simply talking to an attractive woman sitting alone at a bar. She flexed, "I don't care if I am dancing naked on the bar, when I say stop it means stop." She remained at the bar, and the men didn't talk with her again, though they turned to catcalling a woman who walked into the bar.

Dana told me that it was only the next day that she realized she stopped short of doing everything to check the conduct of those men. She failed to ask the manager of the bar to insist that the harassers leave. Instead, she reduced her options to staying and being uncomfortable, and risk further insult and imposition, or leave. When women are customers, we have a self-authority to make these requests. The third option, the one she was a day late on considering, is the option she realizes should have been her first-choice decision.

A final consideration. A three-stage pattern of conduct has emerged from the deluge of disgusting accounts of high-profile men confronting allegations of sexual harassment. First, they emphatically deny the allegations. Second, they effusively disparage the accusers. Third, they egotistically decry the scope of media coverage. Their absence of remorse and contrition should completely revoke our consideration of redemption of their status and restitution of their reputations, and that revocation should last as long as the scarring impact of the harassment, assault and rape that festers as a living wound in the memory of their victims—permanently.

Neither should we afford any forgiving sentiments to the self-serving, public-evading, accuser-dodging, press-release apologies they belatedly issue. When Louis C.K. offered his apology, he referenced being in a position of power because the women subjected to his perversions "admired him". What C.K. completely fails to comprehend is that his power doesn't come from their admiration. It comes from something much more base, and far more overwhelming—the privilege of being male. This privilege is not an insidious assumption, covertly employed through all institutions, sectors and branches of society, to mandate and maintain an advantage for a majority population. It is a privilege enforced by brute. The fear that girls grow up, and that women live with, is rooted in one simple truth: boys and men have more muscle mass than girls and women, and have a proven history of using it to inflict harm on girls and women. Period. Full stop.

I am considering one concession to Louis C.K. During his apology, he mentioned his accusers and other people, entities and productions he hurt by his behavior. In so doing, he apologized to his manager, David Becky, "who only tried to mediate a situation that I caused." He apologized to the man who was complicit in hiding his deviant displays. No doubt unintentionally, C.K. indicted Becky in the court of public opinion. He named a name.

I hope any future town hall telecast will do the same.

The Antidote To Office Gossip

Alicia Bassuk/Claire Lew

Harvard Business Review 11/11/16

SARA*, THE CEO OF A software company, had recently fired an employee. In a heartbeat, gossip about the who, how and why of the termination began spreading through the office grapevine like chicken pox in a kindergarten classroom.

The copy-room commentary was flat-out false. But the buzz quickly infected her team with a rumor that more people were on the chopping block, even though this was far from the truth.

How did the gossip get to that point? Why do workplace rumors happen in the first place? And what can be done to prevent them?

---

* All names have been changed.

Up to 90% of conversations qualify as gossip. That means it is almost certain that you are pretty regularly a rumor initiator or enabler, listening without deterrence. And it's not just cafeteria and hallway whispers that contribute to the problem: Nearly 15% of all work email can be categorized as gossip.

To be sure, not all gossip is bad for an organization. But the kind that poisons rapport, maligns reputations, and contaminates cooperation is what you need to take action against. To do this, it's important to go back to the basics and understand what gossip really is: casual and unconstrained conversation, about absent third parties, regarding information or events that cannot be confirmed as being true.

Gossip is born out of uncertainty. When we are uncertain, we are inclined to make assumptions. Why? Uncertainty creates a knowledge void that must be filled with actual, or in many cases artificial, information. The antidote, of course, is open and honest communication with your employees. Here are a few strategies to try.

Give Them The Low-Down

A big change in a company—firing a top executive, shutting down an office — can be a tripwire for explosive speculations if the change isn't communicated clearly to employees. Because uncertainty creates a knowledge void, be sure to quickly fill the void with facts before suspicion becomes "fact." The more quickly you spill the beans, no matter how painful doing so might be, the less likely people are to start panicking.

For example, before seeking to acquire another firm, Joe, the CEO of a midsize consumer packaged goods company, gathered his team and revealed the company's financials in great detail. Next, he outlined the process for acquisition with a well-defined timeline. In the following weeks, rather than counterproductive chatter clamoring through the ranks, Joe saw his team become more cohesive, rallying together to pull the company through a challenging and transformative time.

Get The Scoop From Employees

Katrina, the COO of an international software company, made a decision to terminate her entire sales team over the course of a year. It was a move she knew would send the company into a frenzy. To mitigate this, she regularly asked questions *before*, *during* and *after* the process. She wanted to know:

- How did people feel about the decision?
- Was there anything she should be doing differently as the COO to make the transition smoother?
- How was the leadership team handling the aftermath?
- Was there anything people wanted to know about the situation that they didn't already know?

By asking questions early and regularly, Katrina signaled to her employees that she valued their feedback and that they were encouraged to become invested in the process. As a result, she squashed the development of widespread negativism within the company, even during a difficult time.

Always Wear White

Gossip can ruin team cohesion as flagrantly as slinging mud on a white suit. When trust is sullied, rancor, animosity and misgivings can turn a culture of cooperation into a mosh pit of dysfunction. To "wear white" means to be mindful of mudslinging—and the more you know someone, the less likely you are to malign them. So, encourage employees to get to know each other as people, not just coworkers.

You can promote workplace fellowship by:

- Sponsoring company events and outings.
- Conducting creative icebreakers at the beginning of team meetings.
- Hosting a one-on-one lunch with a different employee each week.

Be A Role Model

Employees look to their managers as role models and messengers of organizational values. It's one thing to insist on conduct based on mutual regard and high character; it's quite another to demonstrate it. Ethics and empathy should be the tandem directive for conduct. If you model integrity in what you say and do, your employees will likely follow suit. Consistently communicate your expectations in written policies, verbal exchanges and meaningful actions.

In addition, you can block gossip by sticking to the facts—what verifiably was said, done, or occurred—and by being direct. If someone is giving you an earful, let them know you will not participate. If they persist, excuse yourself from the conversation.

Gossip has been undermining relationships since the beginning of time. You can diminish its impact by eliminating knowledge voids, fostering feedback, encouraging relationships beyond coworker consideration, and modeling the conduct of mutual regard.

After all, grapevines are better suited for making wine.

How To Build Company Culture?

Medium 3/19/19

A FEW MONTHS AGO, WHILE FLYING across the country, I decided to binge on my favorite basketball podcast, *The Woj Pod*, hosted by Adrian "Woj" Wojnarowski from ESPN. The season's end retirement of the Miami Heat's Dwyane Wade was on my mind, so I selected his February 2017 interview. Then I closed my eyes to download the in-depth insights I reliably receive from Woj.

Less than 15 minutes into the interview, I was pulled from my podcast meditation, by a word that is like intellectual candy. Woj, who often asks his guests to talk about the identity and culture of their teams, prompted Wade by stating, "People talk about culture and it's a cliché they throw around….but very few places is there a real culture…"

Wade responded, "Yeah, the standards don't change no matter who comes in and out." He then did a crossover stepback on any further discussion of identity and culture, and launched into a conversation about Head Coach Erik Spoelstra's philosophy of staying in the present. Following his lead, Woj moved on and so too did my eager intrigue about the subject of culture.

The next interview I listened to, also conducted in February 2017, was with then Los Angeles Lakers forward Julius Randle. Woj again brought up the topics of identity and culture. Eighteen minutes into the podcast, Randle said, "I just feel like culture is important...having an identity as a team of who you want to be is really important." When Woj asked Randle to define culture, he described the three pillars of the team's approach to defense—one of which he could not recall. He added, "It means, like, who you are. Your identity. We knew every night we wanted to be top 10 in the league in defense."

Randle makes two excellent points—both identity and culture are important. But even while making those points, he is unable to comprehensively describe the specifics of either. That is no slight to Randle. The words *identity* and *culture* are as difficult to detail and define, as they are pervasive in the parlance of team sports. They are often mentioned by players, coaches and general managers when discussing the interpersonal dynamics of a team. What is usually conveyed is a cliched list of attributes: having a winning culture, selflessness, a leave it all on the floor work ethic, player development, strong defense and aggressive play. These attributes are desirable for any team seeking success. But with every team asserting them, they are not the distinguishing characteristics of any team's unique identity or culture.

When I hear discussions about these words, I'm left more with an impression than an understanding. Teams desire a self-evident distinction that unifies everyone with a singular intent—winning. The concept of *team*, at its core, is defined by that distinction, unity and intent. This applies whether you consider the Navy SEALs or the Seattle Storm.

The NBA has a rich history of players whose identities have left an indelible mark on the league. Walt "Clyde" Frazier's tailor-made swag converted stadium corridors into fashion runways players stroll across, in route to the locker room. Allen Iverson imprinted the hip-hop lifestyle onto the NBA perhaps more than any other player. Rasheed Wallace was known for his volcanic volatility. John Stockton played with the stoic severity of a drill sergeant. The outlandish flamboyance of Dennis Rodman stood in stark contrast, to the barbershop precision of Mark Price. And if you juxtapose the larger than life, superhero persona of Shaquille O'Neal against the never back down, giant slayer bravado of Nate Robinson, it's clear to see that the height of identity is measured by the ruler of self-determination.

Similarly, the NBA is replete with cultural influences from a multinational roster of more than 100 players from over

40 countries. The league operates in two North American countries with very different cultural profiles. Its 30 teams are based in 30 cities, each with its own patchwork quilt of diverse cultures. NBA preseason Global Games are played in Israel, China, Italy, Germany, Russia and the Philippines. Regular season games are played in Mexico, Japan and the United Kingdom. Scouts recruit globally. And one team is spearheaded by the first ever African-born individual to become a GM and President of a franchise.

Individual identity can be easily displayed, and cultural diversity can be as easily seen. However, without clearly defining what actually distinguishes one team from any other, the words *identity* and *culture* are reduced to being locker room platitudes and media catch-alls. They are spoken with the connotation of something that is actual and verifiable, but that becomes assumed and vague in explanation.

Culture is the one aspect of an enterprise that it has total autonomy to determine. Culture and identity, when specifically defined and established, are the two greatest lures for top talent. The uphill climb of this challenge is as open-shot obvious, as it is open-lane overlooked. Words like *identity* and *culture* are similar to words like *trust* and *hope*, in one regard. Because they are so widely and commonly used, most people think they have an absolute and applicable understanding of them. But I have pressed thousands of people to precisely define them, and they can't. My efforts to help them do so has led me to one irrefutable truth: words form thoughts that lead to actions.

The inability to concretely define words leads to the inability to form concrete thoughts that lead to concrete actions. For example, in basketball, a "screen" is an action, a blocking move set by an offensive player on a defender to free a teammate to shoot, pass or drive. Tell someone who has never played the game before to set one, and stand-still confusion is what you're likely to get instead.

Likewise for *identity* and *culture*. They don't have to be ill-used words lobbed at interviewers like ill-timed alley-oop passes. They can be simply defined, so they can be caught by thought and dunked into action. To really understand a word, go to its origin—as any Scripps National Spelling Bee contestant ever covered by ESPN would advise.

Identity is about sameness and oneness. Sameness describes what is distinct and different. Sameness is why groups are formed from individuals with like-minded perspectives and pursuits, which makes them comparable to and compatible with each other. Oneness is why individuals construct, project and defend their individuality to distinguish themselves from everyone else. Magic Johnson and Kareem Abdul Jabbar are individuals who will forever be identified as Los Angeles Lakers (sameness), and as individuals who possess wholly distinct and different personas (oneness).

Culture means to prepare, develop and guard the growth of people, and to harvest their creativity and productivity. This is why culture is an all-encompassing phrase that includes the language, customs, cuisine, arts, institutions, beliefs, morals, music, lifestyles and achievements of a specific people. These aspects are evidence of a way of thought and conduct, which led to their preparation and development. They are guarded by traditions, values, standards, principles, rights and rules. And they are the yield of what has been harvested from the hearts, minds and efforts of many people. The Red Auerbach era of the Boston Celtics defined a culture that yielded championships, as did the Phil Jackson era of the Chicago Bulls, and now during the Steve Kerr era of the Golden State Warriors.

Identity is who you are. Culture is how you live. Pick any two people in Paris and who they are can be easily discerned, but both live the Parisian way. Relative to sports, "who you are" speaks to the collective mentality of a team conveyed in demeanor and personality—its style of play. In that identity is the physical expression and projection of self-distinction, who the players express and project themselves to be on the floor, as a team, distinguishes the identity of the team. When Toronto Raptors' Head Coach Nick Nurse speaks of having an "entrepreneurial" coaching style, it is clearly expressed and projected in the style of play of the team—everyone doing everything all the time to win. *Entrepreneurial* aptly describes the league-wide shift to a positionless style of play.

Ambiguity about a team's identity results in a haphazard and jerry-rigged system, to support that ambiguous identity. It also makes the possibility that apathy, dissension and losing will more likely define what distinguishes the team.

The "how you live" part of that premise speaks to the operation, function and social engagement of the team as an entire organization. From president to GM, to coach to player, to trainer to equipment manager teams need to establish an environment with prevailing attitudes, stated expectations, defined qualities of character and uniform standards of conduct that systemize and ritualize everything from operations, to practice, to play. This is why people speak of the New England Patriots "way", or the San Antonio Spurs "way". You need only listen to Tedy Bruschi or David Robinson talk about their former teams, to know that they not only valued and adhered to the cultures of their teams, but continue to advocate for the "way" that continues to distinguish them.

Incoherence about a team's values, principles and ethos all but guarantees that the personnel of that team will be unable to marshal a consistent and cohesive effort for excellence. It also cancels out one aspect of culture that all but guarantees it actually exist.

Brad Stevens, in his March 2014 interview with Masslive, breaks down his understanding of culture. "I don't know if we'll be able to measure it until we're down the road, even standing here at this time next year. But I think the one way that you can measure it is, the guys are still connected. Even with all the change that we had midseason, I've been really pleased with how connected they are."

This aspect of culture, that prevailing and enduring connection, is something that both Stevens and Wade allude to, as proof of the presence of a substantive culture. **Perpetuity**. When the pervasive, defining culture of a team perseveres through changes of personnel, statistics and identities, it means that it is the expected and accepted way of conduct for that entire organization.

Perpetuity requires a leadership mandate from top to bottom. It must foster a total buy-in effort directed by a singularity of purpose. Both effort and purpose must be resistant to any competing interest, and dismissive of any superficial commitment. This mandate is established to maintain the standards, atmosphere and shared goals of excellence that players and staff invest in, rely on and uphold.

This is what protects the innermost sanctum of the team, its locker room, from toxic personalities, adverse media, undermining tension, destructive dissension, and the exemption and normalization of socially unacceptable, counterproductive conduct. Strong cultures are reinforced when challenged by such problems. Weak cultures crumble.

How can a strong identity and culture be created?

The origins lie with the mission, focus and instruction of an individual with commanding leadership influence, and clear organizational objectives that can be articulated as policy and applied as practice. If a leader's influence is negative, demeaning, combative and duplicitous then these will become the dysfunctional directives for the team. If a leader's influence is positive, encouraging, collaborative and earnest then these will become the functional directives for the team.

Whether the leader is the owner, the president, the GM or the coach, they curate—formulate, authorize, implement and validate practices, routines and systems that institute the beliefs and principles of the organization. Ultimately, a team's identity and culture are the manifestation of the leader's core values, which guide the thoughts and conduct of everyone in the organization.

The applied mandate of the leader must be reliably consistent and equitably enforced, in order for it to become fully adopted and habitual. The habitual behavior of a team reveals the consistency of its capabilities, the resolve of its character, the strength of its cohesion and the adherence of its principles. Ultimately, this will forge an identity that distinguishes a team from all others, and institute the culture that will sustain it.

NBA teams overuse clichés and familiar phrases. Instead, they can do the hard work introducing and repeating a new shared vocabulary that commissions conduct. Just as every football team has its own play book, every team can have its own concepts and terminology for the identity and culture it seeks. If it incorporates and reinforces the objectives of the entire organization through the daily duties of everyone involved, it will codify the maximum development of each individual and yield the maximum benefit for the team. It can preserve, protect and promote the highest motivation of everyone, towards developing the strongest bond for achieving the shared goal. This new vocabulary will become the language of the organization, spoken and repeated with frequency for it to become imbedded in the thought DNA of each player and staff member.

Specific behaviors don't become standard conduct without infrastructure to support it. When standards of conduct are well conceived, well conveyed and well maintained without exception, the behaviors become habits. Policies, practices and protocol can be clearly stated, employed and implemented. Initiatives and events can be periodically sponsored to adjust, improve and correct any misalignment. Interdepartmental communication can be open, constant and cooperative. The needs and requests of the team are addressed with the greatest expediency, to insure that the focus required for excellence and adherence remains sharp.

Every team is at risk of difficult dynamics and problematic circumstances. By engineering 'pillar protectors' to curtail and disqualify counterproductive behavior, poor conduct is unlikely to spread and infect the entire environment of an organization, and impair all efforts for excellence. Drafting clear guidelines about comportment, and assigning and enforcing specific penalties for noncompliance, provides a boundary.

The most helpful guiding question for every member of the team is this: "If everyone in the group suddenly behaved this way, would the team be better for it?" If the answer is no, triage and treat to immediately stop the spread of the disease. Everyone can inoculate themselves with a degree of personal responsibility and accountability that rejects misconduct. Preservation of the culture can supersede the significance of any individual. It's the last line of the wolf pledge in Jungle Book, "…the strength of the pack is the wolf, and the strength of the wolf is the pack." The team is the pack, and each individual's conviction to the identity and culture of the pack is what makes it strong.

When a team is ready to express their identity, and leadership is dedicated to curating a culture, then a team's identity and culture will be distinctly defined and generationally preserved. And when more teams are able to do this, the league itself will evolve with even greater distinction and durability.

Isolation Is Not Iso-Ball

Medium 3/13/19

LAST WEEK, I WATCHED ADAM Silver's interview at the MIT/Sloan Sports Conference, an interview conducted by podcaster, founder and CEO of *The Ringer,* Bill Simmons. As a female sports enthusiast, listening to Simmons can often times be likened to listening to someone with chronic halitosis. I really want to hear what he has to say, but the odor of his persistent relegation and habitual omission of female athletes and fans can be an alienating stench to tolerate. Nonetheless, I used my interest in the NBA's current challenges, to cover my sociologic nose and hit play.

Commissioner Silver has always struck me as a person of great composure, someone whose hand is always firmly on the throttle that regulates his emotion and reason. That's why I found it a bit surprising, though appreciated, that he spoke with discernable emotion when talking about young players and the problem of isolationism, a societal problem affecting youth in general. Through several conversations Silver has had with players, the issue has become one that registers on his radar screen of concern. With a recent focus on player mental health, and the current buzz topic about player happiness, that concern bears directly on the image and entertainment product that is the NBA.

This was the first time I heard the term *isolation* used in sports. Silver used it to describe the psychological and emotional deprivation players can experience, upon joining the league. Feelings of disconnectedness, loneliness and even depression are not uncommon when making the adjustment. I wanted to hear more about this issue. That led me to another Simmons podcast, featuring sports journalist Ryen Russillo.

Well into the discussion, at about the 82-minute mark, Simmons and Russillo brought up the point that players have each other's phone numbers, but that they usually don't spend much time together off the court. Simmons made the comparison that players from 20 years ago "had no choice but to hang out", while players today have technology that isolates them.

The discussion then moves to a guessing game, as Russillo and Simmons select players to evaluate for how, despite their financial and professional success, they can still feel isolated.

They begin with Giannis Antetokounmpo and quickly dismiss him as a bad example because Giannis "seems happy all the time". Next, Klay Thompson, who they also dismiss as a bad example because he "just rolls with everything".

Finally, Simmons and Russillo settle on Andre Drummond. They describe him as a 25–26 years old making $30 million per year, and a "top 5 rebounder; never really had playoff success; people pick him apart online… one of best 50 guys in the league".

Russillo moved the discussion of how this is an example that people don't focus on what is great about our professional situation, but rather about the things that frustrate us. Simmons runs with this topic. He mentions that Kevin McHale always understood how lucky he was to play with Larry Bird but that if they played together in 2019, McHale would be conditioned to think he needed to be the star of his own team. The discussion moved completely past the topic of isolationism, without a trace of deeper evaluation for understanding.

However, Simmons and Russillo stumbled upon a tremendous gem of insight, before burying it beneath the footsteps of their gloss-over exchange. By pointing out that Giannis and Klay were bad examples of isolated players, they unknowingly pointed to a possible reason why. A greater understanding of this reason could provide a solution, to a player-plaguing isolationism that may be league wide.

Financial abundance and professional success do not form a firewall against isolation. The privation it creates can be a mental, emotional and psychological state so consuming that it undermines everything people often associate with "happiness". If the tragic and surprising suicides of people like Kate Spade and Anthony Bourdain don't demonstrate this, nothing will. Furthermore, isolation doesn't discriminate. It will strike the prettiest girl in class, as quickly as it will the gay student outcast. And it can cripple the most powerful linebacker on the field, as capably as it impairs a frail widow.

Cash, cars and championship rings can't sit and have a conversation with you; or wish you happy birthday; or tell you a joke; or introduce you to the person you fall in love with. Friends, and more significantly, family can. This is what Russillo and Simmons stumbled upon, what Klay and Giannis have in common. Both live near their families of origin. Both have talked publicly about this. And both attribute much of their feelings of support to this.

The March 8, 2016 podcast on The Woj features a discussion between Adrian Wojnarowski and Klay Thompson. At minute 33 during the podcast, Woj says "The way your family pulls for each other in your careers...not every guy has that kind of family support; there's a lot of guys who go through this very alone. Once you get to this level you realize how rare it is what you have...and what you have as a family, to have that kind of support system." Thompson responds, "Yeah, oh definitely.

It's something I don't take for granted…Being drafted in the Bay worked out so great because I'm far enough from all my friends and family but close enough that they can come see me anytime they want…I always love having my parents up here…and my little brother when it's on his off season.…I spend my off season with my big brother working out…These are the people I grew up with and I can trust them the most…I know they have my best interest…".

In the TNT documentary *Finding Giannis*, sports agent Giorgos Panou explains that when Giannis came to America "he was vulnerable, scared…He didn't want to go home. He was alone." Once he was able to move his family to Milwaukee, Giannis bought a home, so they could all live together. In a NBPA interview from April 2016, Giannis talks about how he spends weekends going with his family to Chicago.

Nearly every player entering the NBA is moving out of their family home, away from the city and neighborhood they grew up in. They move onto a street they've never seen before, in an area mapped out by avenues, drives and boulevards they don't know. They are also leaving the friends and family that comprised the social universe of their interactive world. Even those players who enter the league from colleges and universities are leaving campuses and dormitories that gave them a reliable geographic familiarity, and provided them with friends and teammates who were face-to-face accessible. They move into cities where tens of thousands of people can identify them with pointed-finger recognition and the expectation of instant friendliness, but not a single face in the crowd really knows who they are, or cares much to beyond the request for a selfie or a signature.

Their new found, multimillion-dollar purchasing power and stadium-cheering lifestyle won't erase their separation anxiety; nor will it accelerate their emotional maturation and growth; nor does it reduce their dependency on and longing for loved ones. Neither will it reduce their spotlight pressure to perform; nor expedite their camaraderie with new teammates; nor bring them comfort when looking at a city filled with new "neighbors" they have no personal history with. Add to this the social confinement of social media that many players supplement their hours with, and it's not difficult to imagine that the world presented to them as their oyster quickly becomes a clam that closes in on them.

Simply keeping players near their families might not be the most feasible remedy. Alternatively, the NBA can create a supportive social infrastructure that substitutes the family support system. The league can do this by employing the *proximity principle*, which states that physical accessibility and immediacy greatly promotes the formation of interpersonal relationships. This is part of the reason most colleges offer dormitory living. When young people leave their families, they suffer when isolated and do better when they live amongst their peers.

There are three quick ways teams can use the proximity principle, to resolve the isolationism their players experience.

Offer subsidized luxury housing near each other. This can be a multiple unit hi-rise, or 1–3 smaller building with apartments specifically designed for their stature and needs. These apartments would exclusively house players. These buildings can be within a short distance from one another (2–3 block radius). The desired effect is to create transition dwelling by grouping people in a similar circumstance with similar backgrounds, for bonding and a sense of community.

Create cohorts to create connections. Enhance the potential for connection between players with more purposeful interaction, when they are at work. Player cohorts can be created amongst new players, rising-star players, veteran players, injured players, or players with a shared interest in leadership, conflict mediation or character development. By creating an environment in which players are talking about meaningful topics such as personal relationships, second-career plans, dealing with injuries, managing life away from the practice facility, or adjusting to a new team (players, coaches, staff) the social connections and support are likely to be maintained when the players go home—especially if they live near one another.

Break bread. Build bonds. The importance of a family meal should never be underestimated or overlooked. When people are gathered around food, it creates a natural time for people to bond—everyone has to eat. For players, the team is family, so team meals don't have to be limited to road trips and bus rides to and from the plane and the airport. Give players the option to return to the practice facility, for group dinners prepared by the team's culinary staff. Menus can even have a "home-cooked" feel, featuring food items and meals they grew up with or are specific to their cultures and ethnicities. Teams can also bring in chefs from local restaurants, and sponsor cooking classes for players at the facility. The collective dining and learning experience can do much for establishing team unity, and for preventing players from developing social patterns and habits that create disconnection.

Various other rituals and activities can be introduced, to provide more frequent social interactions within the team: establish a team WhatsApp group; have a pre-shoot around coffee clutch; get coaches to host meals, movie nights or card-playing tournaments at their homes; set up weekly player-child playgroups for players with children; offer players the chance to adopt a shelter animal and provide pet trainers at the facility for group obedience training; provide a calendar of and provide group transportation to and from the events. Teams don't need a social director to make any of this happen. Just one person in leadership can weave this into the daily life of players, with virtually no additional resources and very little time.

Isolation can erode the will and skill of the most motivated and gifted players, adversely impacting their self-esteem, their performances and their careers. Having a next-level awareness and consideration for the welfare of players can reduce or eliminate that impact. Doing so will no doubt favorably impact the overall success of teams who deem this a worthwhile concern.

3 Ways To Ward Off Toxic People

Oprah Magazine 2/08/17

YOU'VE SEEN THESE PEOPLE. YOU'VE been around them. You may have even encountered them directly. They stand inside elevators, staring at you as you race toward the doors closing in your face. They don't talk; they dictate. They don't conversate; they interrogate. Dread is their wardrobe. Agitation, their favorite color. Goodwill flees when they enter a room. Although talking to them for 30 seconds is like taking a 10-mile hike on a rocky road in wet stilettos, you *can* neutralize toxic people. You just have to identify which type of pestilent personality you're dealing with—and then follow these steps to inoculate yourself from their effects.

Type I: The Toxically Infused

People like this likely spent much of their formative years in environments (households, schools, neighborhoods) where social interactions were often abrasive and contentious. The volume knob for conversations turned from loud to yelling. Patience had a brief life expectancy, and courtesy was virtually extinct. For the Toxically Infused, corrosive communication has become habitual and ingrained. Convulsive exchanges are their normal engagement. They simply don't interpret their conduct as being flagrant and unseemly.

Behaviors: talking loudly in public spaces, imposing on and interrupting conversations, unmannerly speech, inappropriate comments, gratuitous profanity.

The Inoculation: Firm guidance. To defuse the infused, you'll need to think like an uncompromising mentor. The Toxically Infused have not been taught or exposed to the ways of civil etiquette. They have no concept of an "inside speaking voice" and are bluntly unskilled in tact and diplomacy. If you demonstrate you are well intentioned rather than demeaning, they will often act upon the opportunity for self-improvement.

Inform with insight. Metaphors and analogies are great for giving someone a reference model for conduct. For example, if someone nearby is talking loudly and refuses a request to tone it down because they don't think it's a big deal, try this comparison: "I get that, but let me ask you something: Does it bother you when someone blows cigarette smoke in your face? Talking loudly around others can have a similar effect on them."

Type II: The Toxically Complicit

People like this know acceptable standards of conduct. They realize mocking and bullying are bad behaviors but participate in them, cashing in their principles for advancement. The Toxically Complicit view themselves as doing what's needed to survive (and sometimes thrive), and they rarely reflect on or are censured for their insensitivity.

Behaviors: gossiping, status-seeking opportunism, double-dealing hypocrisy, shunning and excluding individuals, condoning by silent consent.

The Inoculation: Demonstrate character. The Toxically Complicit have a moral compass; they just stick it in their pockets and follow the crowd. Be the North Star. Redirect them. Challenge them on being enablers and practitioners of mistreatment, and make their doing so a deal breaker for your respect, rapport and reciprocation.

Give them a moment, and then make your position clear: "You can be someone who steps on people or someone who stands up for them. I'll walk away from you on one but stand with you on the other."

Type III: The Toxically Insurgent

People like this need to be equipped with warning signs blinking from their foreheads. Sirens should sound when they are within range. They are belligerent by choice, staunchly believing the Machiavellian adage "It is better to be feared than to be loved." Disparaging others is like breathing to them—they need to do it to feel alive. No one feels good around them. Everyone wants to avoid them. The Toxically Insurgent keep the threat of a blindside attack at DEFCON level. And like a lead-encased room designed to be impervious to nuclear radiation, their "logic" is equally impenetrable to kindness and sensibility.

> *Behaviors:* soapboxing, condescension, being judgmental, abusive and inappropriate comments, undermining and embarrassing others, hijacking credit for other people's ideas and work, spitefully withholding information to sabotage.

> *The Inoculation: Sin aire, no existe*—without air, it doesn't exist. The Toxically Insurgent act with a scorched-earth policy, so learn to snuff out or douse.

Fire cannot burn without oxygen, so don't give them any. Your reactions and rebuttals are the air this type needs to sustain their flames. Completely refuse to respond to or accommodate them in any way, including isolating them from others whenever possible, unless and until they can conduct themselves with civil consideration. This is like putting a jar over a candle. Poof. Second, be direct, be decisive and then dismiss. Frankly state, with flame-retardant austerity, your objections to their conduct, and document every exchange. Clearly list what your next steps (consult HR protocol) will be to critically curtail their interaction with you.

Do not let toxic people infect your demeanor, morale or self-esteem. With a little know-how, you can boost your psychic immunity against them.

Five...Four...Three... Two...One...Lead!

HuffPost 10/07/17

EVERY PLAYER HAS HAD IT, the five-second hero fantasy of taking the buzzer-beating shot to win the game. Growing up, WNBA and NBA players have practiced it hundreds of thousands of times on slanted driveways, in poorly lit gyms, and in bedrooms with balled-up paper and trash cans for baskets. Each has scripted and narrated the Hollywood moment that would elevate them to legendary status:

> The ball comes. The clock starts. The seconds tick. The pressure builds. Your team watches. Your coach stares. Your bench stands. Your fans wait. The shot spins. The bulbs flash. The net rips. The crowd cheers.
>
> FADE TO BLACK.

The reality is that heart-pounding victories are won in such moments. So are hope-baited seasons and history-making champions. Question: how many players have indulged and practiced that hero fantasy, having made the game-winning assist, the game-winning steal, the game-winning rebound or the game-winning blocked shot? Add the game-winning shot to that list, and you have five actions that can win a game. There are five players on the court. Any one of them can be the hero. Any one of them can do something game-winning.

That way of thinking is team-factored not star-fixated. There will always be one player, who stands out more than others, as being most critical to a team's success. But restricting the possibility of victory to the feats of that one player, reduces by four players the maximum opportunity to win. Case in point.

In 1986, Michael Jordan scored 63 points against the Boston Celtics, in Game 2 of the Eastern Conference playoff, breaking Elgin Baylor's playoff record against Boston of 61 points, set in 1962. After the game, Larry Bird was interviewed about Jordan's performance. He said:

> "I think he's God disguised as Michael Jordan. He is the most awesome player in the NBA."

That night of his record-breaking performance, Jordan and his Chicago Bulls lost in double-overtime, to a Celtic team that prevailed with five eventual Hall of Fame inductees. Boston proved something that game that Jordan later learned, in order to win his six championship titles: *one man will never beat five.*

Championship teams know this. Solidarity is their constant mindset. It is never sacrificed for or sidetracked by an individual's pursuit of glory. It is never abandoned or surrendered by the collective will of the team. The attitude and approach is five for five, all the time, regardless of which five take the court. This has been a proven and unchanged model for success, from the time of Bill Russell to the time of Diana Taurasi.

However, professional basketball has changed dramatically through the years. Women now dunk. Seven-footers shoot three-pointers. Power forwards play point guard. Public service announcements, featuring NBA and WNBA players, address homophobia and domestic violence. Spotting up on the perimeter has replaced cutting through the lane, when defenders leave to double team. Small ball has ended the era of tall ball domination. And the best free-throw shooter in the game isn't a man. Conventional player roles, marketing and style of play are outdated by today's game.

What seems to have changed very little, though, is the dated notion of what a team "leader" is and what "leadership" means. These words are often mentioned during interviews with players and coaches, by announcers and commentators while broadcasting games, and by sports reporters, analysts and talk show personalities on sports shows. What is seldom if ever heard are their meanings.

Traditional concepts, images and expectations of a team leader are of a vocal taskmaster driving teammates to play harder, smarter and better. Since score is kept and scoring determines the outcome of the game, the leader is most often thought to be the dominant scorer on the team. This person is expected to accept and assume the leadership role, and lay claim to the team's identity by strength and force of personality. This is endorsed by use of the terms "his team" and "her team".

A strong and forceful personality can actually be problematic for a team, if the individual is ego-driven and self-absorbed rather than goal-driven and team-focused. The first views teammates as props, for a "me" production. This is about imposing your personality as a dictate, and can have an alienating effect on a locker room. The latter views teammates as an ensemble cast, for a "we" production. This is about utilizing your personality as a resource, and can create a unifying culture in a locker room.

Leadership is behavior, and behavior is governed by a mindset— a way of thinking. Mindset is mentality, and mentality is reality. As you think it, you will act it and your actions determine the outcome of what you do, your reality. How you think and what you think also directs both the path and pace of your success.

To direct means to guide, which means leadership is guidance, and a leader is one who provides it. Therefore, as a leader, your most important function is to set, steer and sustain the mentality of the team with same-page reality. To do this, you must establish the one thing all championship teams have; the one thing that makes every great leader great; the one thing that commits every player, all the time to a game-winning mentality:

Trust—an unshakable, unbreakable confidence in the support of, reliance upon and accountability to others.

Trust must not only be the challenge of the leader to earn. It must also be the challenge of everyone to earn and give in return. To be the guiding behavior of the team, trust must be an all-in, all the time commitment from every player and every coach. And for it to be present in the last five seconds of the game, it must be present in the first five seconds of the locker room.

Every player can benefit from leadership development, and every team can benefit from the leadership development of its players. Doing so would elevate the level of team cohesion demonstrated by championship teams. Why? Leadership development is demanding personal development. The more command of self a player has, the more commitment of self a player can make to the team, and the more application of self a player can make to the shared goal of ultimate achievement.

Not every player and not every team's star has the personality, to be the central figure for imprinting the team's mentality. Player development needs to assess which player(s) has the personality suitable for a key leadership role, and work to enhance that individual(s) accordingly. Doing so will increase the likelihood of team success, by decreasing the likelihood of a player's inadvertent failure to take on that role. For example, Draymond Green is not the dominant scorer on the Golden State Warriors. Neither is he considered the premiere-marquee headliner. That spotlight shines mainly on Stephen Curry, and more recently on Kevin Durant with his MVP Finals performance. But Green is unquestionably the most prominent determiner of the team's intensity, focus and shared will to win. His presence has helped to lead the Warriors to the apex of the league.

Player development can also take a less centralized and more collective perspective about leadership development. Each player has talents and attributes that can be recognized as a standard to excel to (rebounding, free-throw shooting, perimeter defense, passing into the post, conflict resolution, transition defense, court awareness, camaraderie, etc.). Each player can lead the others in the development of their talent and attribute deficiencies, to move everyone closer to a greater level of excellence across the board. The elevation and evolution of the team's collective abilities adds to its formidability. From that collective perspective, each player can resolve to contribute to overcoming the team's most hindering deficiencies, to reduce or eliminate any weaknesses vulnerable to any opponent. This insures that each player contributes to and takes responsibility for the guiding mentality of the team, and trust that each player wearing the same uniform will and is doing the same. Trust wins.

The most crucial moments at the end of a quarter, half, game or season can be won or lost before the start of either. What will determine that outcome, more than anything else, will be the mentality that creates the reality, when the final buzzer sounds. One adage to remember underscores this with perfect sensibility:

There are two types of people in the world: those who think they can and those who think they cannot—and they're both right.

Mentality is reality, no matter which seconds you count. Leadership mentality counts when those seconds matter most.

Throw A Flag On "Violent"

HuffPost 9/30/15

A POLITICAL MAXIM STATES THAT THE truth is nine-tenths perception. The NFL should apply this, to the social perception of its stand on off-field violence. With domestic violence committed by players being the most inflammatory and headline grabbing, the league should heed the perception of one demographic group, with particular concern. According to Scarborough Research, women make up approximately 45 percent of the NFL's fans. With a total fan base of 150 million, that translates into 67.5 million women perceiving the league's message on this issue.

The second game of the September 14th Monday night double-header, played between the Minnesota Vikings and the San Francisco 49ers, represented a missed opportunity to adjust the focus of our social perception lens. The game featured the return of Adrian Peterson, following his 15-game suspension for being indicted for child abuse against his 4-year-old son. While on the exempt list for the suspension, Peterson continued to receive his salary. Though his paid leave ended following his no-contest plea of a misdemeanor charge of reckless assault, it was reinstated after a federal judge overturned the suspension in February.

This truth is but one point of note from the game, regarding the league's messaging on violence. San Francisco 49ers running back Carlos Hyde emerged as the star of the game, ending concerns Bay area fans should have about the departure of Frank Gore. Nonetheless, a relevant concern remains.

Carlos Hyde was also the star running back at Ohio State University. While there, he received a three-game suspension following an allegation of assault against a woman at a nightclub. The incident was caught on tape by security surveillance. Assault charges were subsequently dropped by the woman involved.

Whether any sensitivity training was done with him following this incident, or upon being drafted into the NFL, is unknown to me. If it was, it certainly was not present during his postgame, on-the-field interview with Lindsay Czarniak, the female sideline reporter for the game. When asked to describe his running style, Hyde responded, "I run violent." He went on to repeat this with bold insistence, something he also did while attending Ohio State.

The optics of this would be obvious, were it not for the cultural myopia of the NFL, and to some extent, the social myopia of the league's fan base. In the wake of Aaron Hernandez, Ray McDonald, Ray Rice, Adrian Peterson and Greg Hardy, the league nor his team has not counseled (enough?) Hyde, on the linkage of personal conduct regarding domestic violence and assault against women, to language used in an interview—particularly with a female reporter. This speaks to a truth-perception issue evidenced by an analysis done by ESPN's Outside the Lines:

> Of the 48 players considered guilty of domestic violence from 2000-2014, the league suspended players for only one game or no games in 88 percent of the cases, according to the OTL report. That means that 27 players received no suspension, while 15 players were suspended for one game.

Adjunct to this, fan violence has become as commonplace during many NFL games as the singing of the national anthem. In fact, following Monday night's game between Minnesota and San Francisco, the same game featuring Peterson and Hyde, a Vikings fan was savagely attacked, mob-style, by 49ers fans who took offense to his biased banter. Perception meets truth.

Player and coach interviews offer teams and the league an opportunity to provide game insights and analysis, chalkboard sound bites, support for fellow teammates and compliance with mandatory media obligations. Such interviews also provide a chance to demonstrate an earnest effort at amending the mentality that sponsors the perception problem the league now faces.

I am not naive enough to think that new words can be spoken like magical incantations to suddenly change the culture and mentality that has long defined the NFL. However, old words will certainly guarantee the status quo. Conduct is offspring to thought, and all thoughts are conceived by words. New words, new thoughts, new conduct.

Along with mandating media obligations, perhaps the NFL and its member teams can mandate sensitivity training for its players. At the very least, send out a memo about language and messaging. Carlos Hyde could have been coached about different adjectives to describe his running style like "unforgiving", "unrelenting", "rampaging", "ferocious" or "inhospitable". An amusing euphemism might have made for a better sound bite: "I run like somebody took my lunch money" or "like somebody stepped on my new shoes". Anything but "violent".

I'll spell it out: sixty-seven million, five-hundred thousand woman are watching—and listening.

From Contagion To Outbreak:
The Death Of Leadership

HuffPost 8/9/16

"Napoleon once said, when asked to explain the lack of great statesmen in the world, that 'To get power, you need to display absolute pettiness; to exercise power, you need to show true greatness.' Such pettiness and greatness are rarely found in one person."
—*President Jackson Evans,* The Contender

NEVER HAS A MOVIE QUOTE been more relevant for its time. Given the rare duality it suggests, the presidential nominee of the Republican Party should be seen for his exceptional unexceptionalism. Donald Trump continues to sicken the discourse of the election process, and threaten the life of a party whose president, senators and representatives once collectively saved the nation from its greatest existential threat ever.

Pettiness is a disease of character that targets temperament. Its symptoms are pathological insecurity, inflammatory behavior, rash perspectives, malignant speech and an anaphylactic reaction to truth. Trump is in a state of septic shock.

Like Clostridium botulinum, the bacteria that causes botulism, pettiness is a pathogen to virtue that causes contempt. Contempt is airborne, transmitted by puerile name-calling, denigrating insults and divisive propaganda. If left unchecked, it can rapidly spread before a response can be developed to combat it. I would wager that contempt has infected, afflicted and decimated more people than all other physical diseases combined.

Almost immediately after Senator Barack Obama became the nation's first African American president, the Republican Party unleashed a particularly infectious batch of contempt with a declaration of intent to destroy his presidency. Unfortunately, Republicans were not mindful about containing the contagion. No one bothered to monitor the vital signs of the party.

Soon afterwards, an indication of mutation occurred, and with it came the realization that a scourge was in the making. The Republican Party initially reasoned the Tea Party useful for debilitating Obama, as the upstart insurgents inflamed tensions by disseminating toxic rhetoric. The party of Reagan was seemingly unaware of the highly contagious ideology it had given rise to, and greatly underestimated its potential for outbreak.

The ulcerative dysfunction of our government and the political epilepsy of Republican Party leadership have become obvious consequential ills. Just as a neurotoxin attacks the central nervous system, striking the body with paralysis, contempt has likewise disabled the principles of the GOP. Rather than promote itself as the party of optimistic pragmatism, Republicans have instead become the party of contaminating petulance. It should be no surprise then that Donald Trump has emerged to be its standard bearer.

Years before, David Duke, a former Grand Wizard of the Ku Klux Klan and a Holocaust denier, tested the Party's resistance in 1989. Despite risking political capital on an otherwise insignificant election, both Presidents Ronald Regan and George H. Bush interceded to suppress Duke's candidacy for a state congressional seat in Louisiana. When asked why he came out against Duke and even suggested voting for the Democratic candidate instead, President Bush said, "I did what I did because of principle."

Principle. The Oxford Dictionary defines the word as a fundamental truth or proposition that serves as the foundation for a system, a belief or a chain of reasoning. I would add that principles also serve as the foundation of character, and that the preservation of character depends tremendously, if not solely on one defining attribute: integrity.

Integrity is defined by the reliability of an individual, an institution, an organization or a corporation's adherence to a moral and ethical conviction for conduct. Integrity is also used to describe the condition, fitness and soundness of a structure.

Unfortunately, history provides much evidence that the avarice of power weakens the immunity of integrity. For the sake of the nation's aspiration of a more perfect union, the Republican Party needs to cure itself of its cupidity. It needs to revive its integrity by resuscitating its principles. I offer two for consideration, from one of its own.

Nine-term Republican congressman, one-time vice-presidential candidate and Housing Secretary under President Bush, Jack Kemp once opined that, "The purpose of politics is not to defeat your opponent, as much as it is to provide superior leadership and better ideas than the opposition." He also said, "Democracy without morality is impossible." The principles defined by Kemp seem to be so lofty now, as to be stratospheric in reach for Donald Trump and the GOP. But quite literally, that fate of the nation depends on the Republican desire, will, recognition and conviction to put country before party. Rather than adhering to the petty, disingenuous support of its nominee as an electoral calculation for claiming the White House, the Republican Party, should—must withdraw support from Trump, and immunize itself with a great act of integrity to preserve its existence. This would be an incredibly difficult thing to do, but the aforementioned film provides one more quote to consider to that end:

Principles only mean something when you stick to them when it's inconvenient.

—*Senator Lanie Hanson,* The Contender

How To Deal With a Soapboxer

Harvard Business Review 8/30/16

HAVE YOU EVER WALKED DOWN the street and encountered a squawking, sermonizing windbag shouting to everyone about how they should live their lives? How about the bullhorn-blaring corner preacher? And the all-knowing, sign-wearing doomsday prophet roaring about government conspiracies?

This is called soapboxing, a term stemming from an era when a person would literally stand on a soapbox crate as a stage and scream to the world that he or she knew the right way — the only way—to do anything. Fortunately, on the street you can simply walk by the modern-day version and escape the diatribe.

But what if you couldn't? What if you had to work with that person? What if that person is *you*?

At work, a soapboxer tends to be utterly convinced that his or her view is the *only* view — and vocalizes it. Being near such a person can be unpleasant, annoying and antagonizing. Trying to work with one, especially during a group task, can be alienating and incredibly unproductive. A soapboxer can elevate tensions to the point of completely destroying the rapport of a well-functioning group.

You don't want to be in a room with a person like that. Even more, you don't want to *be* that person. So here are some ways to deal with both situations — starting with how to recognize if you've got one foot (or both) on the box.

Talk to, not at. Soapboxing has absolutely nothing to do with hearing or listening. It is a declarative form of speaking. This doesn't just stand in contrast to the collaborative intent of group decision making; it is in opposition to it. Making proposals is not the same as making pronouncements. If you talk incessantly at and over group members, you're telling them you do not value them or their perspectives. "Talking at" is dictation. "Talking to" is conversation — what a group discussion is supposed to be.

Watch the toes. Have you ever had someone step on your foot? It hurts, doesn't it, especially when they don't have the courtesy or consideration to apologize? This is what happens when people pompously talk out of their area of expertise, or beyond the role of participation they are asked to contribute.

So, don't step on other people's toes. Imposing unsolicited and uninvited opinions in a forceful manner is a sure way to offend others, and eventually it can lead to your marginalization within the group.

Don't beat a dead horse. Soapboxers keep pounding on the chest of an issue well after it has been pronounced dead, the funeral has been held, the hymns have been sung, and everyone has left the grave site. Make a habit of doing this and you'll be left standing alone while the other members of your group move on with the real-life concerns of making or executing a decision. If you want to appeal the group's decision, or if you have a concern that the group is making a mistake, request a short meeting with the leader of the group to speak up one last time — and then put it to rest.

Broker it. The more you assert your perspective, the more irritation you'll provoke. Conflict courts enemies not allies. Group pushback can actually be a moment for conversion, if you redirect your approach. So, ask don't tell. A question is an invitation for consensus. Ask what aspects of your proposal are problematic for the group. Incorporate their concerns, modify your solution, and reduce their discomfort of risk. Narrowly focus your perspective on an aspect of the decision to be made, not its entirety. This will demonstrate that you are accommodating, not domineering and dismissive. The windfall: People will incorporate your perspective into the group's focus, while regarding you as a team player.

Take their order. When you go to a restaurant, you expect to be served by an accommodating waiter who is more than willing to explain the menu, and help you make a decision about selections for an enjoyable meal. What you don't expect is someone who comes to the table, and yells at you about what you should eat. That would no doubt prompt you to leave and never return.

So be accommodating. Instead of bullhorning your opinion to an alienated and irritated audience, try ingratiating your presentation. Point out and explain nuances that help others see the convincing cause of your solution. Start by asking group members to write their main goals on a whiteboard. Next, innovate and demonstrate to them how your solution addresses each of their objectives. If you find ways for many goals to be supported, people will rally around your solution. If you cannot find ways to support their goals, accept that your solution isn't a winner. The same can be done with another person's solution, until the right method is agreed upon.

What should you do if you work with a frequent soapboxer? First, know that they probably either lack the self-awareness to realize they are perceived this way, or they are intentionally soapboxing to get their way. Don't expect them to behave in a collaborative way. Instead, do the following:

- Stay focused on your perspective and keep the group's collective focus on the main topic. Doing this will reduce the likelihood that you will be emotionally triggered and diverted by conflict. Clearly state your views to stay grounded and clear-minded.

- Present an example of decorum for the other group members follow.

- Remain purpose-driven about the decision to be made.

If the soapboxer tries to reclaim the stage, shut it down with a direct rebuttal: "We heard about that point, and now we are considering others."

This person may claim to have the support of someone who isn't in the room. Don't accept this. More than likely, it is a strategic bluff for validation, a duped concession by the other person who lacks clarifying information, or a caving in by the other person who just wanted to end the annoyance. Offset any such claims by reconfirming the groups' decision-making independence, direct person-to-person input and group conversation.

The conference room isn't a stage for proselytizing your team members. And it isn't a legislative chamber to filibuster their intentions. If you want to declare to the world how right you are, pick any street corner and start squawking. If you want to prove you can make a valued contribution to the decision-making process of your group, show mutual respect.

Conduct Detrimental

HuffPost 9/15/15

KEN BELSON'S NYT ARTICLE, NO Foul Mouths on This Field: Football With A New Age Twist, offered encouraging insight into the changing culture of the Seattle Seahawk's, with the team's non-traditional approach to optimizing player performance. I appreciate and applaud the alternative approach described. While teams have proven innovative throughout the 95-year history of the NFL, such innovation has been largely represented via rule changes, training, equipment, offensive/defensive play schemes and game analysis. The coarse-tongued, coach-berating, check your emotions at the door culture of the league has largely remained intact. This approach, one exemplified by the current episodes of Hard Knocks on HBO, gives proof that old-school mentality is hardly considered outdated.

This mentality could also be described as an "ole boys" approach to the game. The numerous and scandalous occurrences of domestic abuse, drunk driving, PED suspensions, player bounties and the air pressure of balls continue to evidence an alpha-male culture that endorses violence, compensates egregious conduct in lieu of performance and often blurs the lines between right and wrong, good and bad, ethical and unethical. It is the latter demarcation that, despite the commendable effort involved, calls me to question the Seahawk's approach—on one point in particular.

Belson's article explained how psychologist Dr. Michael Gervais, "a former competitive surfer turned human optimization specialist", is largely responsible for the altered atmosphere in Seattle. The success of Gervais' approach has other teams calling the Seahawk's, inquiring about the how-to's of replicating his model with their teams—a compliment that should have Gervais riding a wave of success for some time to come.

Also revealed was that Gervais and head coach Pete Carroll have created a performance enhancement business called Win Forever. As a consulting firm, it seeks to instruct and advise other businesses, organizations and yes, teams about the non-traditional methodology employed by the Seahawks. As other NFL teams consider the Gervais/Carroll-Win Forever approach, a question begs me to call an audible. Isn't this a conflict of interest?

Understand that I have no specific knowledge of the Gervais inspired approach being used in Seattle, and forming the foundation of the Win Forever way of doing things. Neither do I have any purpose, intent or cause to impugn the integrity of either Dr. Gervais or Coach Carroll.

However, that a team's head coach and an "outside" advisor can form a business together based upon the very services that advisor offers to that head coach's team is ethically ambiguous, at best.

If Gervais and Carroll are motivated to build a business, then, as a practical matter, how much of their mental focus is directed towards laying a foundation for obtaining other consulting contracts while cultivating their curriculum in Seattle? Relative to fiscal governance, how much of every dollar generated by Gervais, via consulting provided through Win Forever, is leveraged as windfall for Carroll? How does this preserve objectivity? How does the general manager and head coach of another NFL team feel assured that an approach instructed by a competitor, is actually to the benefit of their team? Does this potentially compromise any proprietary concerns a competing team might have by letting Win Forever into its locker room? Onto its practice field? Inside the heads of its coaches and players?

What would be the implications of a head coach forming an injury rehabilitation company with the trainer or doctor employed by that coach's team to service that team's players?

What would be the proprietary infringement concerns of other teams using this company for injury treatment of its players? If an agent represents several players on one team, would it be regarded as good business for that agent to form a business partnership with that team's general manager or head coach, for player representation?

The waters such considerations must swim in are frothy to murky. The Carroll-Gervais connection would do well to do well in Seattle. Such an aspiration would do better in a clearer pool of operation.

A final note: Carroll's commitment to diversity seems to be substantiated by Gervais, if one considers being a non-traditionalist as a barrier-breaking, category-busting distinction. I would urge that such a commitment consider diversity as an insistent opportunity to be more inclusive of individuals from truly different backgrounds, perspectives, personal experiences, cultural affiliations and even gender.

The fields of psychology, performance optimization, team building and leadership development are replete with female professionals. The old school mentality the NFL seeks to amend, and that Coach Carroll seeks to challenge could be altered even further by giving female advisors more earnest consideration. What could be more non-traditional than employing a woman in a male-dominated setting? With that asked, I likewise applaud the league for its hiring of Sarah

Thomas as the NFL's first female official. Kudos also to the Arizona Cardinals for hiring Jen Welter as the league's first female coach. Hats off to the NBA's San Antonio Spurs for recognizing the prowess of Becky Hammon, too.

Experience And
It's importance In Leadership

Medium 9/8/19

L AWRENCE O'DONNELL, HOST OF *THE Last Word* on
MSNBC, interviewed U.S. Representative and Democratic
presidential candidate Eric Swalwell on Thursday evening,
May 2, 2019. During the interview, O'Donnell asked Swalwell the skeptic's query relative to experience for a candidate
campaigning for the highest office. To be specific, O'Donnell
asked, "How important do you think the issue of experience
is, for a candidate for president?"

The context of the question was a comparison between Representative Swalwell and former U.S. Senator and Vice President
Joe Biden, also a presidential candidate. Swalwell, age 38
and now in his fourth term, has been an incumbent from
California's 15th congressional district since 2013. Biden, age

76, began his political career in 1973, as an elected senator from Delaware. After nine terms, he went on to serve as vice president for eight years, for President Barack Obama.

Experience is often thought to be a compulsory requirement for the task of leadership, and to the credibility and selection of a leader. At twice Swalwell's age and having more than seven times the years in service as an elected official, Biden's experience quotient overshadows that of Swalwell's, to the point of invisibility.

Representative Swalwell answered O'Donnell's question, in a manner typical of candidates running for political office. He cited his service on both the Intelligence and Judiciary committees, defending our country from international threats to our national security and to our rule of law. He also qualified his public service resume mentioning his seven years as a prosecutor, and "some of the highest National Security policy experience, aside from Joe Biden."

Swalwell's effort to shore up his bona fides did not exactly address the substantive gist of O'Donnell's question, that being the importance of experience and not necessarily the quantitative degree of it. His miscue in answering this was later underscored by his closing remark, which was a more salient and direct challenge of the value question regarding experience as a qualification. Swalwell concluded, "I also believe that being in Congress for a lifetime, not being in

Washington for a lifetime, also brings a perspective that will bring new energy and new ideas, and a sunny optimism that we can still solve these big problems."

The possibility of new energy, new ideas and a sunny optimism being ushered in by a perspective not hewn from incumbency has merit, as well as appeal. It was an appeal used by Donald Trump, arguably the least qualified individual to ever run for president, when considering the metric of service as an elected official. Given the pessimism that tracked his campaign, and that continues to mar his presidency, the merit aspect of that possibility seems less convincing.

However, the merit of experience as a qualifier for leadership is also questionable. Consider that there are currently 435 members in the House of Representatives, with an average of 9.4 years in service. Similarly, there are 100 members in the Senate, with an average of 10.1 years in service. When totaled, the aggregate years served in the House is 4,089, and in the Senate, 1,010. That is a combined total of 5,099 years, slightly more than five millennia. Given the caustic divisiveness of our national discourse, and our present difficulties and dilemmas regarding environmental and nuclear treaties, trade and tariffs, gun violence, climate change, health care, infrastructure, domestic and international threats to our form of democracy, it would be reasonable to speculate if experience has any real value at all for leadership.

It does. The more germane perspective is what kind of experience?

Experience is the knowledge gained from observing, encountering or doing. An investment of time is required to acquire the applied comprehension, competence and skill that determines it. Everyone who has ever sat in classrooms, endured basic training, attended seminars, sweated through scrimmages or practiced hours to capably play an instrument knows this. Practically speaking, the more you do anything, the greater your aptitude and proficiency for performance becomes. But this generalization like most generalizations must yield to the nuances of conduct, and the variables of circumstance.

I consider experience to be of two types: primary and secondary. While both are significant to leadership, one is more fundamental than the other.

Job experience is what is generally thought of, when evaluating leadership. We are inclined to believe that individuals with more time vested in a job, rank or role are better qualified to lead others. The history of their day-to-day, year in-year out application of training, situational recognition and task familiarity makes them better suited to head an agency, department, organization, company or team. This defines secondary experience.

I have seen many examples, in virtually every profession, sector, industry and arena of life that secondary experience IS NOT an indispensable prerequisite for leadership. Otherwise, people with no political background would never unseat an incumbent or defeat a more tenured opponent in an election. Rookie athletes, entering a locker room of veteran players, would never immediately be deemed or expected to become leaders of their teams. Film school neophytes would never direct doyens of the industry to critically acclaimed performances. And young adults, barely out of high school, would never command squads and troops through the life and death circumstances of actual combat.

What enables them to do this? Preparation—the actions, procedures, methods and training done to become ready and able to undertake, execute and perform a task. Preparation defines primary experience, the trial and error operational knowledge gained from learning, training, rehearsing, testing, proving and planning.

Military and law enforcement personnel undergo hundreds if not thousands of hours of tactical training, situational instruction and role playing before being approved for active duty, and assuming any rank of command.

A political candidate can be well schooled in coalition building having spearheaded a venerated non-profit organization, or played an integral role in building an entertainment enterprise, or worked as a community organizer.

Athletes practice the last-second play over and over again for years in parks and playgrounds, before ever executing a buzzer-beating, game-winning score as professionals.

From the hours, days, weeks, months and years spent in preparation, comes the activation and refinement of many of the attributes that comprise leadership. Without primary experience, the many moments for secondary experience are meaningless.

Leadership can also spontaneously occur from seminal moments that override the need for primary and secondary experience. Such moments extract extraordinary conduct from ordinary people who are pressed into form, by climactic circumstance. With attributes spontaneously activated these rare few people are instantly transformed into leaders, capable of doing the superhuman or uncommonly heroic act:

> In 1955, a seamstress named Rosa Parks did not practice or plan for the moment she decided to rebuff the Jim Crow dictates of Montgomery, Alabama. But in that moment, self-determinism, intent and courage christened her as the flash-point person to initiate the modern-day Civil Rights Movement.
>
> Nothing could have ever prepared Thomas Burnett, Jr., Todd Beamer, Mark Bingham, Jeremy Glick and Sandy Bradshaw for encountering hijackers aboard Flight 93, on September 11, 2001. But with the possibility of targeting the White House, the Capitol Building or a nuclear power plant, their self-sacrificing heroic moment of leadership to thwart the hijackers spared the lives of many hundreds, if not thousands more.

Candidates running for any office, would do better to convince the electorate of the scope and effort spent on their preparation for leadership, rather than tout their accumulated years in office. Seniority does not always equate with possessing deft judgment; having a crisis-management aptitude; being highly skilled and inclined towards coalition-building; or demonstrating the competency, expertise and vision for realizing a new and better reality. Moreover, accruing years in service doesn't always insure that an individual has gained this knowledge. What needs to be assessed is not how long you've done it, but how well you can do it. To follow anyone, people need to be convinced of this.

When Should You Fire a "Good Enough" Employee?

Alicia Bassuk/Jodi Glickman

Harvard Business Review 5/25/15

CRAIG*, A VP OF INVENTORY for a food packaging company, had always been a high performer. He had been with the company three years, had a reputation for taking an innovative approach, and had good relationships with his team. Craig's boss, Louise*, had come to count on Craig for his expertise and experience. During a factory move, however, Craig began to disappoint. He took many personal days during the move, and Louise found herself stretched thin covering for him. To add fuel to the fire, when Craig was asked to onboard several new employees, he pointed to a lack of HR leadership as an excuse for delaying the process indefinitely.

---

* *Craig and Louise are based on real people, though their names have been changed*

So, was Craig's performance an anomaly or a canary in the coal mine? After giving Craig direct feedback, Louise watched in dismay as he failed to take the initiative she had hoped for. Now she was really in a bind—how much credit did she give him for past performance? Should she settle for "good enough" going forward, or was it time to let Craig go?

The decision to terminate an employee is never easy. Firing someone you've worked with for years, especially someone you know and respect, is often excruciating. Even the most experienced managers lose sleep over it. It's almost impossible to take the emotion out of what is a very personal decision—even when it's a decision that makes rational, economic sense on paper.

So, amid all of these conflicted feelings, how do you know if your employee is still an A-player worthy of another chance? How do you know when enough is enough?

Let's assume you've done everything right up until this point. You've delivered honest and constructive feedback about your employee's performance. You've set realistic goals and objectives for him or her to meet, with a concrete timeline to follow. And of course, you've asked your employee for his or her input around how to improve performance as well. From a management perspective, at least, you've done everything in your power to set expectations, give guidance, and empower your underperforming employee to step up to the plate.

If that still doesn't work, what then? Ask yourself the following three questions to help shed light on the right course of action:

1. **Is your employee meeting the responsibilities listed on his job description?** This is the baseline, and yet many of us don't refer back to a job description after we've completed the hiring process. Neither do our employees. But by revisiting a job description well into an employee's tenure, a manager can assess how aligned the employee is with the job description. He or she can then have a meaningful discussion about each part of the role, re-calibrate the employees' priorities, and revise the job description, as needed. If the employee's performance isn't matching with the current or revised job description, it is time to terminate.

In Craig's case, was he good enough to keep things moving along at the factory? Yes. Was he performing all of his responsibilities with excellence? No. Was he maintaining his role as an exemplary leader of the organization? No. Unless there are extenuating circumstances, an employee who isn't doing his job brings everyone down. It's not fair to you, it's not fair to them, and it certainly doesn't do your clients or customers any good either.

2. **Can the market offer you a better employee at the same price?** Louise was especially trigger-shy because she hadn't done any succession planning for Craig's

role. How hard would it be to replace him? How much time, energy and resources would she need to invest to find someone with the skill, talent and dedication she needed?

We all know that replacing talent is an expensive proposition. Data shows it can cost anywhere from 20% of one salary to upwards of 200% of one's salary to replace an executive. So, there's no question that the hiring process is daunting but, with few exceptions, everyone is replaceable (as much as we'd like to think otherwise).

Craig was a valued employee with a solid history of performance, yet his eventual replacement brought a fresh pair of eyes, diverse thinking, and a powerful professional skillset. In the end, markets are efficient and talented employees looking to progress forward in their careers are abundant. Managers need to keep this reality in mind, even though it can be hard to see in the moment.

3. **If the employee resigned today, would you fight to keep him?** This is the final litmus test. By reframing the question this way, you will candidly address your internal debate: How would you feel if he left you? Devastated? Then maybe the relationship is salvageable. Relieved? Then it's time to show your employee the door.

Louise ultimately realized she was hanging onto Craig because he was the devil she knew. That's not a good enough reason to retain a good-enough employee. Like Louise, you will find another employee who will exceed your expectations and make you question why you waited so long to act in the first place. And Craig? He has been free to move onto another job with a better fit. While it may be incredibly difficult in the moment, it's often better off for everyone in the long run.

About Last Night's Game

HuffPost 2/11/16

WHAT DOES A SHOTGUN HAVE to do with Hail Mary? Can a naked bootleg be shown on network TV, on Sunday afternoon? If he drops a dime, do they stop the game so he can pick it up? Aren't they afraid somebody is going to slip on it?

Listening to sports terms and slang being tossed about like cards dealt across the felt of a game table can leave you feeling like the only sucker in the poker game. If you're a woman who always folds her hand during gabfests about sports, then you're never in the game when it comes to what is often male-dominated office chat. Rather than marginalizing yourself during these conversations, get your head in the game.

It may surprise you that you are more interested in professional sports than you think. Do you have a functional knowledge of the rules, plays, scoring and player personnel? Don't worry. You're still holding chips. Are you intrigued by discussions about leadership, relationships and culture? How about astronomical salaries? Race relations? Domestic violence? The hero worship of pop icons by children? Good. Make a bet. These issues and themes are the many threads that make up the fabric of professional sports.

Critically acclaimed and Emmy award-winning shows like the *30 for 30* documentaries on ESPN, *Real Sports* on HBO and *60 Minutes Sports* on Showtime are devoted to eye-opening and revealing analysis of a myriad of social and cultural topics woven into the textile of sports. Viewing such shows will help you focus on topics that are relatable to you. After getting hooked on HBO's *Hard Knocks*, I decided to finally follow up on a deferred ambition—to coach the coaches of professional sports teams. There isn't a replay junkie or a couch coach in your office that won't want to chat about whatever is covered by these programs.

This past summer, during a car ride with a couple male colleagues, I mentioned my dismay about police violence against unarmed citizens, including tennis star James Blake, a Black pro tennis player who was attacked by police while standing in front of his hotel during the U.S. Open. This led to a half hour discussion about topics ranging from racial profiling to cultural stereotyping, Second Amendment rights, conceal and carry laws and Trayvon Martin.

Employing broader social-cultural relevance beyond trivia discussions will move sports chat to your comfort zone. Change the game. Make professional sports your interest and gain the home court advantage at your office. And when all else fails, use the phrase that professional athletes use with the media—"They came out to play."

How The
"Average American" Sees It

HuffPost 7/18/16

THE AD COUNCIL'S VIDEO, "WE Are America/Love Has No Labels" featuring John Cena, had already gone viral weeks before the sports world's equivalent of the Emmy's aired live. The ESPYs opened with the full version of the PSA, championing a sentiment of patriotic unity and equal value for all Americans, in the wake of the tragic events of Orlando, Baton Rouge, St. Paul and Dallas.

The video set the stage for sentiments and political expressions made by several athletes who addressed the audience, keeping those in attendance and television viewers across the country focused on the role sports and athletes do, can and sometimes choose to play when influencing social consciousness. To his credit, Cena spoke with the "I am everyman" credibility reminiscent of frontline leaders of social justice causes decades ago, the kind of credibility a team of forensic scientists would not be able to find amongst our political leaders today.

Cena's message was moving and salient on many points, particularly as it progressed to his "close your eyes for a second" challenge, when viewers were asked to picture the average U.S. citizen. As he began to reconcile the "average" image being conjured in the average mind, Cena speculated:

> "So, the chances are the person you're picturing right now looks a little different to the real average American."

He went on to deliver statistics about America's citizen profile, facts I am sure were surprising to some: 54 million Americans are Latino; 40 million are senior citizens; 27 million are disabled;18 million are Asian; 9 million are lesbian, gay, bi or transgender—more than the entire population of the state of Virginia (and 40 other states, as well). How many sitting in the Microsoft Theater and around their television sets knew that almost half the country belongs to minority groups? I have a daughter who is a standout at Ultimate Frisbee, but I had no idea that 5.1 million Americans play it.

One demographic statistic Cena stated was lost on the reality of the evening, an inequitable irony given that it was the first statistic he offered:

"There are 319 million U.S. citizens; 51 percent are female. So, first off, the average American is a woman. Cool, huh? Is that what you pictured?"

What followed from that opening video was a male-centric amnesia to that truth. Only three of the award presenters, Lindsey Vonn, Danica Patrick and Skylar Diggins were women—four if you include Billie Jean King's tribute to the late great Pat Summitt. This paltry ratio was a theme continued when considering how many women graced the stage as award recipients, and the scant imagery of female athletes in the many video montages paying tribute to great athletes and great athletic performances. You would have had to been paying close attention to the "honorable mention" style announcements of award winners leading into commercials, to have realized any additional award recognition granted female athletes. Nearly 78 percent of the awards and honors given at the ESPYs went to men, who as John Cena noted by deduction make up 49 percent of the nation's population.

Cena can't and shouldn't be held responsible for the production choices made by ESPN, but he had numerous opportunities to comment on this disparity in his comments and sketches. So too can be said of the many male athletes who dominated the ESPYs, especially given how several of them felt comfortable using the ESPY pulpit, to address the latest police shootings of unarmed African American men and gun violence.

One week before the ESPYs aired, Serena Williams defeated Angelique Kerber to tie Steffi Graf with 22 Grand Slam titles, and taking another chisel strike to etch her image onto the sports world's Mt. Rushmore of greatest athletes of all time—female or male. Twenty years after first stepping onto the court as a pro at 14, she still has a physique that looks like it was engineered by geneticists. And at an age when most male and female athletes wheelchair themselves into the retirement home of former glory, Serena still dominates and dismisses her peers. To look at her, she could knock down Mt. Rushmore. Yet, she failed to be nominated for best female athlete, proving worthy only of a few screen images, and a blurb mention of being recognized as the best female tennis player. This is where I not so unapologetically insert Bill Simmons.

Were it not for Abby Wambach receiving the Icon Award (alongside Peyton Manning and Kobe Bryant), and images of her heading goals into the back of her opponents' nets, memory of the U.S. Women's National Team capturing the World Cup last year (remember the ticker-tape parade?) was just a blur. That achievement distinguished that team as the only team from any nation to have won three Women's World Cups. Their back story approaching the ESPYs—being denied the right by a federal judge to strike for improved wages and work conditions prior to the already plagued upcoming Olympic Games in Rio. The women's national team earned $2 million dollars for winning the 2015 World Cup. The previous year, the men's national team earned $9 million dollars, while failing to advance beyond the round of 16.

There were no female nominees for this year's best play award. I Googled "best female sports play of 2016". The first two entries were about the hottest female athletes. ESPN doesn't have a single listing on the entire first page of the search.

Stanford University won the Capital One Cup for best Division I men's college athletics program. The prize: $200,000 for student-athlete scholarships. Not a sigh or expression of disappointment or embarrassment could be detected by the audience, only applause. Four weeks earlier, one of Stanford's male student athletes, Brock Turner, morbidly raped an unconscious woman by a dumpster. Obviously, the men's athletic program was not disqualified from consideration for the grant, due to the actions of one of its male athletes.

I could point-counterpoint several other categories, but some balance is due. One of the evening's more redemptive gender-equity moments came when Sgt. Elizabeth Marks was given the Pat Tillman Award For Service. After serving as a combat medic in Iraq, and suffering debilitating injuries to both hips, Marks persevered through agonizing surgeries and rehabilitation to once again be declared "Fit For Duty". She is now a world-class paraswimmer, and ranked No. 1 in the world for breaststroke. She also racked up four gold medals at this year's Invictus Games.

Abby Wambach spoke admirably about being herself, a not too veiled inference to never denying one of her core identity traits, her sexuality. She also addressed the income, marketing and opportunity disparity suffered by female athletes. All the more reason I found Breanna Stewart's acceptance speech for best female athlete to be particularly courageous. As a rookie, playing for the WNBA's Seattle Storm, she risks much for being so outspoken, in such a moment, about such an issue. Doing so demonstrated that wage and work condition equity is not just a cause for female soccer players. My urging is that Stewart, and other female athletes from all sports, accept my efforts, and others like me, to help them coalesce for parity with their male counterparts. That the nation could soon be electing its first female president should make such a moment more insistent.

My interest in this issue was provoked after attending the ESPNW Conference in Chicago, this past April. The exploits of female athletes were well presented in impressive videos showing their talents and prowess. Many speakers—reporters, athletes and corporate sponsors addressed the current state of women in sports. I was further spurred by a study presented at the conference regarding gender bias in sports fans, a bias that extends itself to media coverage, marketing promotion, franchise support, working conditions and compensation. That ESPN could sponsor such an event, and not comprehend how its cursory portrayal and inclusion of female athletes at its own award show speaks to a rational disconnect, begs for a moment of self-awareness.

ESPN should be more sincere about the message it uses to intro its own award show. More sponsors should leverage their support for gender equity. More female athletes should find their voices, and proclaim their 51 percent representation. More male athletes should lend their voices to amplify that call. Then, hopefully, next year's ESPYS will be more reflective of the "average" American.

Flexing: #MeToo, Too

Medium 7/19/19

MARK YOUR CALENDAR. IN OCTOBER, exactly two years after their game changing article was published in the New York Times, Jodi Kantor and Meghan Touhy's book, *She Said,* will make its debut. Many people are hoping it will fuel another phase of the #MeToo movement, launching it towards fundamentally and permanently revolutionizing the response to sexual harassment and gender disparity, in the workplace.

The truth, as most will admit, is that women and their allies are still at a loss, for how to more comprehensively and effectively deal with disrespect and devaluation in any interaction. The systemic problems institutionalized by gender politics remain inordinately complicated to navigate, expose and address. This doesn't mean they are impossible to solve. Many women are coping, but coping is not and should never be the ultimate goal. Nearly two years of global attention has not proven sufficient enough, to decisively rectify the indignities women suffer daily in their workplaces.

Six months before the Harvey Weinstein story broke, I wrote an article for Oprah Magazine, about the way I handled a drunk man who bothered me while I was having a drink with a friend. I used a technique called *flexing*, which means to define your value at all times, and to defend it at a moment's notice. Women began reaching out to me from across the globe, asking for advice about what to do when confronted by demeaning and harassing conduct, those willful acts of disrespect they daily tally in their conscience: moments when men mansplain, take credit, rob opportunities, interrupt, condescend, exclude, intimidate, stand too close, creepy-flirt, grope.

These are the same moments that cause women to freeze, feel embarrassed and self-doubt, often resigning them to walk away feeling disempowered. Worse still, many women self-implicate and justify a response or reaction that protects the antagonizer. Equally distressing is the ritual of reenactment that follows, when women mentally and emotionally replay the offending incident repeatedly, with the hindsight courage that drafts the ideal response and reaction in ways they never do real time, in the moment. This recurring ritual has an increasing depreciation on self-esteem, making the likelihood of self-preserving conduct in the future all the more unlikely.

I responded by launching a series of workshops for women and their allies, from coast to coast, to share non-confrontational techniques that de-escalate the emotion that cause women to have self-forsaking moments. The three-hour sessions ended with participants feeling uplifted and compelled, which is difficult to guarantee when women are swapping stories about the menacing behaviors of men.

One concept that many women found cathartic is having a forensic understanding of how they got to this undesirable place they never selected, approved or legitimized. That "how" often has its origins with the process of gender indoctrination, which begins in early childhood when girls learn that self-expression means to internalize doubt; while boys learn that self-expression means to externalize aggression. In the words of Audre Lorde, women are "taught to respect fear more than ourselves...We've been taught that silence would save us, but it won't." With repetition, this becomes the engraved and expected social intercourse between men and women. Even more detrimental, it becomes male entitlement.

An entitlement, as it is basically understood, is a right to claim a benefit or privilege, or to exercise a license for conduct supported by moral standing or legal authority. This is not the same, when we speak of having an "entitlement mentality". Here, entitlement is a belief that you are inherently deserving of special treatment or exceptional privileges, simply because it is your prerogative or desire to want them and not because you are morally or justly deserving of, assured of or prescribed for having them. This is what whites claim relative to blacks, that they are inherently deserving of power and authority, as an arbitrary premium for being white. All racism is predicated on this, with exclusivity. Likewise, this is what men claim relative to women, that they are inherently deserving of power and authority, as an arbitrary premium for being men. All patriarchy is predicated on this, with exclusivity.

This chronic *doubt-aggression dynamic* learned via gender indoctrination instills within men the notion that their desire is an enforceable right. The coercive consequence of this is that it prods women into making emotional, intellectual, mental, psychological and physical concessions that undermine their own interest, advancement and in some cases, safety. These concessions become the implied conduct that signal to men that they can act as they do, unchallenged and with an accepted entitlement. Woman talks to man, man barks back. Woman backs off, man gets what he wants. We, women and men, learn that an explicit expression always trumps an implicit reaction. This dynamic is patterned from the outset, when girls talk to boys.

The workshops offer women and allies a forum to relate their professional challenges. In the first minutes, participants are asked to describe their basis for attending. Initially, there is a reluctance or inability to be forthcoming, and to answer candidly and collectively. A smattering of responses trickles out and are cautiously generic: "I want to learn new tools"; "I'm looking for opportunities for professional development"; "I want to hear about the experiences of other women".

Then I ask them to share examples of sexual harassment or gender disparity they are experiencing, and in tandem I narrate the doubt-aggression dynamic. This inevitably brings about a remarkable moment in which women code switch. With a sudden calibrated sense of urgency, hands shoot up as women become eager to share their specific accounts of unwanted behaviors. They begin to speak rapidly and openly to one another, wanting to maximize this rare opportunity to focus on a topic that has been vexing them.

Only the most egregious offenses are revealed, and no one gives names. Repeatedly, women speak of yielding to men; or giving them the benefit of the doubt by creating narratives that men are unintentionally perpetuating gender politics; or making allowances that men are blind to the repercussions of their actions; or downgrading the indignities suffered as not being significant enough to warrant redress. To this last point, participants can be quite adamant about wanting to differentiate between lesser infractions and those that are undeniably flagrant. They want a scale to grade a range of misconduct. This scale allows them the grant of redemption, to salvage and preserve relationships with male colleagues they deem less offensive and are essential or unavoidable for interacting with.

All of these behaviors are the concessions I previously referred to and are what I call *default disorders*. An examination of the term yields the intended use of it. Default means a failure or neglect to act or perform. It also means having a preselected option, when no alternative option is listed. Disorder means the lack of arrangement or a state of confusion. It also means a condition that upsets and disrupts the normal health and function of the body and mind. These definitions are exactly the outcomes of gender indoctrination that women live as their realities. When we experience situations of disrespect, we often fail to act with self-affirmation (define your value) and self-preservation (defend it), in the moment and instead revert to the behaviors we have been conditioned to respond with. And when we are in these situations, we are often disabled by a paralyzing confusion regarding how best to respond, which results in a circumstance that is detrimental to our well-being, not just our careers. One of the goals of the workshops is to discover and define as many of these default disorders as we can.

I got a sense, when engaging the participants, of how women handle these challenges at work. I identified the most common categories of tricky work situations, and how ill prepared and ill equipped women are about responding to them. Historically, because many women opt not to oppose misconduct, there are few convincing examples that doing so works. Those that become known are judged as being exceptions to the norm, and consequently not replicable.

Just as we can be taught a technique for saving the life of someone who is choking, I teach participants techniques to save themselves or other women when they choke in moments of being disrespected in the workplace. And as success of the Heimlich maneuver is measured by the person's ability to resume speaking, the success of flexing is also measured by a woman walking away resuscitated by the power and authority of her own voice.

Unlike other techniques recommended in these situations, the primary aim of flexing isn't to terminate the unwanted behavior, though that is always an intended outcome. This goal is secondary to how capacitated the woman feels in her response. Consistently and insistently acting with this capability is what brings about a desired change. Every great social movement has proven this. The young adults of the Student Nonviolent Coordinating Committee (SNCC), who challenged the Jim Crow status quo through the Civil Rights Movement, trained themselves primarily to have the unrivaled courage to confront violently hostile bigotry on its own turf, and to do so without violently responding. It was this capability and daring that eventually aided in the culminating act of the Movement—passage of the Civil Rights Act of 1964.

In every workshop, there comes a moment when most participants resist the concept of flexing. There are two parts to this resistance. Part one is something that plagues all groups that have been historically marginalized—a negative identity focus.

This is an injurious outcome of a caste system indoctrination, which results in disparaged groups incorporating disparagements into who they are. From this identity focus comes the development of a concurrent conduct of self-sabotage, as it forms and fosters a less-than mentality as a core component to identity. And no greater truth exists than this: you will never create a greater-than reality, from a less-than mentality. Any introduction of a new identity construct challenges the old, and people are reluctant to move away from who they are towards who they can be, even when they realize that adherence to who they are undermines their reality. For women, a shift in identify focus often times seems even more insurmountable than countering the mistreatment of men.

Part two is the fear of reprisal. With the daily reinforcement of the doubt-aggression dynamic, paranoia becomes the perspective of survival. The thought of standing up to a man at work immediately triggers trepidation of payback. As was borne out in the workshops, whether consciously or not, women don't even consider the possibility of defending their value. They design all interactions to minimize the risk that such a moment will arise, and in doing so create a self-fulfilling prophecy of disempowerment. Women legitimately worry that flexing may cause men to ratchet up their microaggressions in both frequency and intensity. The resulting internal dialogue becomes: "If I stand up for myself, is it going to anger him even more?"; "Will he become vindictive, if he feels unfairly accused?"; "Will he lash out at me, if he becomes embarrassed?"; "Will he undermine me, if he has to protect his reputation or career?" Rather than preparing themselves for those reactions, like the "good girls" they are taught to be, women instead spare men from those feelings. They prefer the devil they know. This more equates with picking what level of hell you want, instead of electing the possibility of being in a heaven of your creation.

By articulating their concerns about male backlash, workshop participants inevitably unite against me. Though they are disheartened by not having solutions for their workplace woes, they become riled and accuse me of being Pollyannaish, or acting irresponsibly for suggesting they risk their employment and careers in this way. This pushback is quite visceral, as each participant expresses a personal reaction to a perceived personal jeopardy. They feel alone in acting to counter misconduct, and that the solitary soldier of a just cause will never defeat the army of an unjust intention.

Simultaneously, they will all agree that not challenging this conduct is tantamount to subsidizing it. So, my first effort to mitigate the backlash is to propose they reason and retain an irrefutable axiom: the more you subsidize poor conduct, the more poor conduct you will get. This holds up whether you're in the workplace, at home, in a mall or at a bar.

My next effort is to guide them to examine and acknowledge their willingness to value the reputations, careers and financial prospects of denigrating men more than they are willing to value themselves. I urge them to establish a line of demarcation with respect to their own value. Essentially, this means to establish within yourself, an absolute boundary of imposition that you will not allow anyone to contravene. With the acceptance of this comes a moment of transformation, which is a vastly more profound and permanent experience of perspective shift than a common understanding of change. I convey this in the workshop, with a simple demonstration.

I move a chair from one location in the room to another. I also reposition it, turning it on its side and face down. With each change, whether in location or position, I ask the participants what I am moving. They answer, obviously, a chair. Exactly. Though I have changed its location and position, I have not essentially changed what it is. I suggest that I can also paint that chair and change its color, or add cushions to it, or reupholster it with a different fabric. No matter how I change its appearance, it is still a chair. This is often what happens with the concepts and language of gender disparity and our response to it. From decade to decade and generation to generation, we can change our focus and scope of conversation about it, its outward appearance as a social issue, without any essential and elemental difference in our response to it or the reaction of men to our response.

My intended point is that to create such a difference, women need to think beyond change. A transformation is a process of alteration so evolutionary and absolute, that what becomes can never again be what was. The butterfly can never again be the caterpillar. The transformation of how women self-identify, value and defend themselves is what will profoundly and permanently revolutionize the workplace—and society.

With this realization, comes my next effort, which is to get women to understand that the same unity they demonstrated in their pushback against me, is the unity they need to take to the workplace to transform it, collectively. This must become a shared and supported effort. Though Rosa Parks initially acted alone against the segregation of the South, it became an entire city and then a nation that galvanized and magnified the dimension of her protest with exacting results. When women are prepared to do this, the desire of their intention is as inevitable as the rising and setting of the sun —or the United States Women's National Soccer Team winning a World Cup.

Lastly, one other crucial realization emerges from these work-shops. There is one thing that women feel much maligned for, but it is the very thing they need to rely on to enable themselves to flex. At the same time, women recognize that they need a better understanding of how this one thing is regarded by men and more importantly, how to adapt their use of it more advantageously. The one thing—feelings.

Women regard "feelings" as valued and informative emotions that not only convey vulnerabilities, detect threats and alert dangers, but also appraise a current state of mind and the quality of interaction. In this sense, feelings are intuitive tools than enhance survival and aid in community building. When women say to men, "I feel", or ask "How do you think that makes me feel?", they are relaying a self-awareness perception, or inviting a discussion about the cause-effect impact of what they are experiencing.

Gender indoctrination instructs men to think differently about feelings. They are taught to interpret them as psychological tells, the signs and cues that divulge indications of strength or weakness. Men are also taught that feelings are inflated reactions that offer no practical, constructive or strategic value for input. Combining the two instructions, men are led to conclude that feelings are irrational disclosures of vulnerability, and nonessential obstructions to reason. It should be no riddle then that patriarchy has likewise judged women as being irrational and nonessential. We are, after all, emotional creatures whereas they are rational beings.

Through the workshops, women are able to comprehend that when men experience women conveying and expressing their feelings, it can be a signal to either act against them with aggression to gain an advantage, or to be completely dismissive of them for having judgment incompetence. The foundation of this is laid for men in their childhood, when they are taught that masculinity is, in part, defined by the denial and rejection of pain, and that femininity is, in part, defined by the confirmation and valuation of it. This is further extrapolated to mean that admission of pain is a weakness, and weakness is to be exploited. This not only desensitizes men to their own emotional awareness, but it also impairs their sensitivity to empathetically recognize and react to it in others. Phrases like "Big boys don't cry" and "Man up" are frequent reinforcers of this emotional detachment.

This emotional differentiation between women and men is not breaking news to women. What is different, as evidenced through the workshops, is a desire for women to make their enhanced understanding of this, an application for their inter-action with men. This is most serviceable in the language we use gender to gender, when signaling emotional exchanges.

Men can be very emotional, whether what they feel is exuber-ance or anger. But rather than discussing their feelings, men simply display them—facial expressions, gestures, voice volume, body posture. In the workplace, to the degree that they do employ some safeguards for emotional restraint it can be found in how they code phrase emotional expressions. Men are less likely to use the words "feel' or "feelings", but instead will camouflage feelings as aspects of reasoning by saying things like "My reaction to that is…", or "The course that sets us on is…", or "Where that leaves me is…". When women hear such phrases, they can gain insight about the emotional disposition of men in those moments. Women can also adopt similar language to better position themselves for actualizing the reality they want for a gender-neutral environment.

The ultimate outcome of the workshops is to transcend empowerment, because to be empowered speaks more to a feeling of potential than it does to a conduct of actuality. Without an understanding and application of how to effect transformational conduct, that feeling can dissipate to dejection or be lip serviced, waited out and arbitrarily ignored by the inexorability of patriarchy. At the level beyond empowerment lies capability. When women are instilled with and fortified by the concepts, know-how and abilities for a new conduct, they not only feel eager to engage in it, they feel ready and able to. That will lead us to the day when our daughters, granddaughters and nieces will flex not as an extraordinary act of social or political assertion, but as a normal, self-preserving behavior. And when their female peers and male counterparts witness it for the first time and inquire, "How did you know to say that?" or "Who taught you to do that?", they will be able to tell them that my mother, grandmother or aunt taught me to flex, when I learned to tie my shoes. To define your value at all times and defend it at a moment's notice should be as basic an instruction as that.

The Rhythm of Rectitude

Medium 9/9/19

PARADIDDLE. IT'S A WORD I learned late in life, but one that has directed my life for as long as I can remember remembering anything at all. A paradiddle is one of the most basic patterns for drumming.

I had a decisive moment several years ago, when my basic pattern became strikingly clear to me. I interviewed for admission to a liberal arts university. My high school admissions counselor told me not to bother applying, one of the reasons being that I didn't have a 4.0 GPA. But I was fortified by self-determination and fail-proofed by my first business suit.

Plucky, perceptive and persistent, I sat in that stale Admissions Office for my interview. I remember being asked, "How will you manage your life ten years out as a professional, who is also a mother?" It was 1989. I was a few months away from recognizing that question was inappropriate, and three years away from using email. Projecting forward to 1999, with the unjaded view of my 17-year-old self, I explained my vision of a world in which everyone can do their work their own way. Years later, that vision resembles what the gig economy is offering more of. Paradiddle, tap-tap, I was admitted to the university.

From the moment I could reason, I began marching to the beat of my own drum. That is not the once boastful claim of a pretentious and precocious child, who delighted in defying and disqualifying adult omnipotence. I was the daughter of immigrants from Buenos Aires. Much of my formative life was spent observing and absorbing, inquiring and learning, practicing and improving.

From childhood, the cadence of adamant curiosity has timed my march through life. I recall hearing it clearly, during the only time my parents ever sat their four children down in front of the television. The momentous occasion—the Camp David Peace Accords. That event sparked a particular fixation for me, that being the character and conduct of leaders. I became engrossed by why and how they do what they do, and who they have to be to do it. I wanted an architectural understanding of their hearts and minds, with the thought that one day I might be able to design and build better concepts and applications for leadership.

I continued on at that university, determined to create a job from my fixation. Again, dissuasion tried to march me to a different beat. In my third year, a staff member at the career office deterred me from applying to the Chicago Business Fellowship at Booth Business School. Why? Because all past winners were economics majors, and I was not. After being awarded that fellowship, I set out to learn the tools and techniques I assumed leaders were being taught in business schools.

During orientation week, all first-year students were divided into small groups to compete in the "Dean's Challenge", a pre-gig economy new venture challenge. My team members viewed my idea as too progressive to win the contest and refused to explore the concept. I joined a more receptive group, and our team won. I invited the team to join me to pitch one of the judges, Michael Thomas, the President of First Chicago Bank, to hire our team as consultants. They scoffed at the idea that he would consider us neophytes as consultants and stayed back while I made my pitch. The boardroom was daunting. I was dauntless. I got hired.

Long-shot challenges have been the slingshot launches that pitched the trajectory of my professional life upward and outward. I don't credit the impertinence of audacity for being able to pursue them past doubters and detractors; nor do I charge it to an extravagant opinion of myself. I attribute it to something I realized long ago. I am not suited for conformity.

From childhood on, the stipulations of prevailing attitudes always made me feel like I was being intentionally shoved or tripped. Arbitrary constraints and deterring expectations threw me off rhythm and caused me to stumble out of step with myself.

Discovering that discomfort was an identity-defining moment of self-awareness. My incompatibility with conformity wasn't triggered by an experience of gender bias, or an incident of immigrant disparagement. Nor was it introspectively conceived as a rejection of civil norms, or a rebellious disregard for discipline, or a defiant resentment of authority. Its origins had a deeper and more fundamental rooting. What I felt was innate not intentional. I could no more dismiss it from who I am, than I could my own genetics.

Consequently, complying with a presumption about my destiny always felt like self-betrayal. My unwillingness to reconcile that meant being unwilling to subsidize the predisposition of others. By default, I was able to do that because of my two most intrinsic traits. I have always been prompted by insistent curiosity and spurred by restless creativity. To seek, question and challenge is not the invitation of conformity. Nor is imagination, originality or change. Those efforts are the guides and demands of self-determination.

I not only wanted to know "what", "why" and "how" but also "what if", "why not" and "how come". My motivation to know drove me past apathy and alienation, without internalizing either. And my fidgety mind was constantly deconstructing, drafting, conceptualizing and reinventing most nearly everything I observed. What resulted was the development of a steadfast loyalty to self, born of a mindset that would not allow me to forsake my interest. It also instilled within me an unyielding conviction to principles, which protected me from compromising who I am, what I believe and what I wanted to do. In other words, what enabled me to resist and withstand the rejections of conformity was integrity.

I understand that word to mean the cohesive strength of what firmly bonds to the point of solidity. This is why integrity can be used when describing the strength of a weld, the stability of a bridge, the reputation of an organization and the composition of someone's character. Each of these examples has a bonding agent that creates its integrity: the soldering compound of a strong weld; the tightly fastened bolts of a stable bridge; the reliable observance of ethics by a reputable organization.

What is the bonding agent of character's integrity? The certainty of self. This is what adheres self-knowledge to self-awareness— the recognition of who you are to the realization of who you are not. This bond seals the resolve of belief in yourself, and this belief is the conviction of conduct, which provides you with the ability to be true to who you are.

My certainty of self encouraged me to decline the advice of my high school counselor, and the guidance from a staff member in the career office at my university. It also bolstered me to win a contest and to pitch a bank president. And it furnished me with a crucial insight, one that daily taps out the cadence of my self-determination: Limitations should be discovered, not predetermined.

As I previously mentioned, a steadfast loyalty to self is one aspect of integrity. The other, an unyielding conviction to principles, provides the daily directives that fortify your resolve to resist conformity.

Principles are the codes of conduct we live by, formed from the values we hold to represent our ideal self. They provide standards that serve as the metrics we use to measure our character, and to gauge the character of others. They establish the resolutions of self-preservation, those guidelines of behavior we follow to define and defend our identity. And when they are objectively reasoned, they are transferable across any generation, culture or social setting.

The character windfall of integrity is extremely rewarding. Amongst its many benefits, three are most notable:

- **Self-possession.** This is a level of demeanor demonstrated by being fully accountable for and in control of your feelings and behaviors. It is completely unaccommodating to the internal conflict, thought annoyance and clouded conscience caused by any challenge or dilemma confronting your principles. It is also impermeable to the doubts, dissuasions and disparagements of others.

- **Self-validation.** This is more than an affirmation of self-value. It is a confirmation of your worthiness and of your authority to act in your best interest. Engaging it means increasing the likelihood that you will attain the goals set by your self-determination, and that you will never be influenced by the pessimism and cynicism of others.

- **Personal accord.** This is a degree of self-confidence that goes far beyond being sure of your abilities and intentions. It means acting with the agency to execute on your terms, in everything you do. Doing so will yield outcomes that are more meaningful and fulfilling to you. Even if your efforts result in partial achievement or complete failure, you will not incorporate that result into your identity. The contentment derived from the full application of who you are will allow you to reconcile setbacks and adversity—without being defined by them. You will not be plagued by regret or persecuted by the guilt of failure.

Despite the benefits of integrity, many people find the lures of conformity to have a stronger draw. There are three that are particularly powerful in their appeal:

- **Accommodation/Acceptance.** A sense of belonging is amongst the most compelling of human desires. So too is the desire to not be targeted for mistreatment. Adapting to the disposition of those in the majority; or capitulating to the preferences of those who are dominant almost always ensures admission into a community of interest, or an exemption from being maligned.

- **Risk avoidance.** This means more than having an aversion because aversion has a variable for assessing a gamble. Avoidance has none. It is an absolute ambition to eliminate any exposure to the responsibility of initiative. It wants to completely elude any possibility of being associated with error. And it seeks to shun any potential of being marginalized, for acting beyond the norms or contravening expectations. Independence operates without a safety net. The uncertainties, doubts, fears and liabilities that accompany it often prove too overwhelming for most people to undertake.

- **Personal gain.** History is awash in fame and fortune stories about people who are willing to compromise or forsake themselves; and adulterate or abdicate their principles in order to curry favor, gain an advantage, secure a promotion, receive a gift, obtain a raise or attain anything they are willing to value more than their integrity.

Conformity necessitates a measure of self-deception, which replaces the certainty of self with moral ambiguity affixed to a veneer of identity. It also requires the silencing of the inner voice that will protest for listening to its truth.

Integrity mandates an unyielding devotion to self-preservation, and to upholding the principles that determine its character. It also amplifies the inner voice that directs true self, on its path for actualization.

In life, you have to decide what cadence to follow. I'm still beating my drum.

Acknowledgements

MY CLIENTS AND FRIENDS ARE my greatest teachers. The complexities and nuances they have shared are what fuels my writing. I will save my specific acknowledgments to them for my leadership philosophy book.

Deep thanks to those who made meaningful contributions on my writing journey:

The Op-Ed Project for mentoring me for my first published opinion piece. Jodi Glickman for giving me the co-authorship and introduction to her editor at Harvard Business Review. Gretchen Gavett, my editor at Harvard Business Review, for her ongoing receptivity to publish my unique perspectives. Mamie Healey at Oprah Magazine for her astoundingly brilliant editing. Kali Evans and Tiffany Dufu for your introduction that led me to Libby McGuire and Casey Ebro, who offered me my first book deal. Jodi Kantor and Ron Lieber for showing me and the rest of the world how writing can influence.

And my editor and mi alma, Michael Laurence Tyler, for teaching me that to write is to think.

About the Author

ALICIA BASSUK IS A LEADERSHIP & performance advisor to individuals and teams internationally. Bassuk provides clients guidance in maximizing individual effectiveness, optimizing team cohesion, and shifting cultures. Her clients have nicknamed her a CEO whisperer, work shrink, executive muse, Yoda, Chief Inspiration Officer, and drill sergeant. Clients include the NBA, McKinsey & Company, Salesforce, Christie's, United Nations, NAACP Legal Defense Fund, Sienna Capital, The Rockefeller Foundation, presidential appointees, world class artists and executives in the sports and entertainment sectors.

Bassuk is an online contributor to the Harvard Business Review, Oprah Magazine, HuffPost, and CNN. She was named as one of the Top 100 Leadership Speakers of 2017 by Inc. Magazine's LEADX.

Bassuk holds an MBA in Finance and Marketing from University of Chicago Booth Business School where she was a Chicago Business Fellow and conducted research at the Center for the Study of Urban Inequality. She also holds a B.A. in Political Science from Wesleyan University where she led the Latino student group and played lacrosse. Bassuk is certified in mediation through Northwestern University School of Law.

Bassuk holds dual citizenship (USA/Argentina), and has lived in Buenos Aires, Tel Aviv, and Honolulu and Chicago. She is the President of the University of Chicago Latino Alumni Board, is a member of the Economic Club of Chicago, and serves on the Board of Harlem based Futuro Media Group.